A PASSION FOR JOURNALISM

A Passion *for* Journalism

A newspaper editor writes to his readers

James H. Smith

NEW ENGLAND COLUMNISTS SERIES

PLAIDSWEDE PUBLISHING
Concord, New Hampshire

ISBN-13: 978-0-9755216-4-9
ISBN-10: 0-9755216-4-0
Library of Congress Control Number: 2005933175

Designed and composed in Adobe Caslon Pro
at Hobblebush Books,
Brookline, New Hampshire (www.hobblebush.com)
Printed in the United States of America

Cover photographs: Color photographs by Chris Angileri,
Record-Journal; black and white photograph by Paula Miller,
Hartford Courant.

Published by:
PLAIDSWEDE PUBLISHING
P.O. Box 269 · Concord, New Hampshire 03302-0269
www.plaidswede.com

I dedicate this book to Jacky Smith,
my muse and my editor.

Contents

Introduction

by
Bill Breisky

Life on this planet is troubling, exciting, uplifting, sad, happy, horrifying, beautiful. If a newspaper is supposed to reflect life and if you are reading a newspaper that does not portray horror, beauty, happiness, sadness, excitement or trouble—if it doesn't uplift you and make you laugh or make you cry—what kind of newspaper is that? It is an irrelevancy at your doorstep every morning.

—James H. Smith, in a 2002 column

IF YOU BELIEVE the First Amendment to the U.S. Constitution "goes too far," and you don't wish to hear any arguments to the contrary; if you feel that newspaper editors have no business criticizing the policies of local school principals, librarians or police chiefs; if you applaud when your government reduces public access to official information; if you're not concerned that fewer and fewer Americans under 40 pay much attention to current events or to the quality of the news outlets in their communities; if you half-wish that newspapers would go away so you could give your full attention to your iPod . . . then this collection of Jim Smith columns probably isn't for you.

But if you believe that a community newspaper should reflect its community back to its readers, warts and all; if you believe that "news" shouldn't be defined for us by government bureaucracies; if you applaud the watchdog role of the press—making a noise when elected officials forget how things should work in a democracy and when the public's right to know is threatened; if you are grateful to former Supreme Court Justice Hugo Black for reminding us that "the government's power to censor the press was abolished so that the press would remain forever free to censure the government"...then you're going to like what Jim Smith has to say on these pages—or most of it, at least.

Yes, but who, you might ask, is Jim Smith?

Jim Smith is a Connecticut Yankee.
Born in 1946 in upstate New York, where his father edited a small weekly newspaper, James Herbert Smith says his parents "were great influences on their four sons. We were raised in a two-bedroom flat. We were a family of modest means. They bequeathed to us open minds, inquisitive natures, respect for differing views, and a commitment to truth, reality—what is real and how we can make it better."

He won the American history/citizenship award in the eighth grade, and majored in American history at SUNY College at Brockport and earned a master's in humanities/writing from Wesleyan University. He taught history in high school for a while, but became a full-time journalist, and a resident of Connecticut, in 1971.

For the past 14 years, Jim has served as executive editor of the *Record-Journal* of Meriden. (In August 2005, Jim was named editor of the *Connecticut Post* in Bridgeport.) He and his wife Jacky live on a hill in Meriden and work several feet apart in the *Record-Journal* newsroom, where Jacky is an assistant managing editor and an editor of Jim's column. "The only time anyone in the newsroom might see us as husband and wife, rather than editor and editor," says Jacky, "is when we walk out the front door together to have lunch. (Yes, we like having lunch together at least once a week, but more often than not we're eating at our desks.)"

Jim Smith is a newspaperman to his marrow.
The columns collected in this book are testimony to that. They also make clear that his passion for journalism and his passion for supporting our First Amendment rights are indivisible.

"The First Amendment," he says, "is just so utterly, absolutely basic to what America stands for. If newspapers don't make that argument, if we don't help educate the public to the value of our rights and freedoms that, my God, so many men and women have died for, who is going to make that argument?"

He believes in asking tough questions, and in insisting that his reporters do the same. He believes in filling his newsroom with people who are not "one vanilla flavor," and in defending his reporters when they are attacked for pursuing tough stories.

As for precisely when his passion for journalism developed, he declares, "I knew even before I knew. I found my journal from college recently and found I had written this down in 1966, by historian Clinton Rossiter: 'One basic liberty. Freedom of the press—the uncontrolled and uncensored exchange in print of ideas, information, arguments and accusations—is in many ways the essential political liberty. The effective conduct of free government is dependent upon the existence of a free press; the fortunes of each seem always to rise and fall together.'"

When he was nominated for the New England Newspaper Association's Yankee Quill Award four years ago, his boss, fourth-generation publisher Eliot White, declared him to be a "champion for a free press, open government and fighting corruption and government abuse"—an editor who "fights for truth, justice and the American way."

Jim Smith is a sporty guy.
The newspaper job he now holds, he maintains, is the best job in the world—"next to being the starting catcher for the New York Yankees."

The first dog in his life was "Yogi"—a little mutt named, he acknowledges, "after Mr. Berra."

(But the thing about baseball, Mr. Berra maintained, is that you can't think and hit at the same time, whereas Mr. Smith has discovered that you *can* think and write at the same time—which is one reason why Mr. Smith opted for writing.)

"He wears his pinstripes well," says *Record-Journal* publisher White, who has ventured to Yankee Stadium many a time with his editor.

Jim is a former basketball player and coach. A former sports editor. A lifelong teller of fish stories. (He fishes on Canandaigua Lake, in upstate New York, "where my family has been for six generations.")

Jim Smith is "Bip."

That's what his grandsons, Tyler and Scotty, call him. Love for grandchildren, he testifies, is "one of the greatest things ever invented."

"As much as journalism is the air we breathe," says his wife Jacky, "the most important part of our life is our family. Jim has turned our yard into a playground for our grandsons. There's the big sandbox he made and painted green, alongside an old rowboat right on the grass. He built a tree fort with ladder-like steps on one side and a slide on the other.

"Not many people have a leprechaun platform in their front yard, I bet. Jim built one in the arms of a Japanese maple, then wrote a story for Tyler about how the leprechauns made it while he napped. In the backyard, Jim built a storage shed, which is for adult gardening tools. When Ty heard about this, he interpreted 'storage shed' as 'story shed.' Bip thought that was a great idea, so he painted the words 'story shed' on a big old turtle shell, put it over the door, and placed a big stone slab in front of the door. He and Ty sit there and tell stories."

A favorite story is the children's book, *Good Night, Gorilla*. Because, says Jim, "it's about freedom."

Jim Smith's boss is "the reader."

For those who read his columns—even those who don't always like what they read—the most important thing to know about Jim Smith is that "he works for the reader." Not the editor above him on the table of organization, or the publisher who pays his salary, but the reader.

The author of that statement is the man who gave Jim his first full-time newspaper job, on *The Hartford Courant* in 1971, and who has been his mentor and best friend for more than 30 years—Reid MacCluggage.

"Many years ago as his editor," MacCluggage recalls, "I pulled Jim off a story he'd been on for a long time. He wanted to stay on the story because there was more the reader needed to know, and I wanted him to move on. He didn't speak to me for more than a year. As I learned, Jim doesn't work for anyone higher than the reader. He's pretty stubborn about that."

But by no means does he patronize those readers he seeks to serve. A great many of his columns go against the grain. "Jim's columns on freedom of the press and free speech," says MacCluggage, "go to the heart of who he is. Jim stands with the people even when they offend the community with unpopular speech. He stands for their right to speak as freely as those whose opinions are embraced by the community."

So, one might ask, does editor/columnist have any bad habits?

"Of course not," he declares.

Jacky Smith begs to differ.

"He insists on climbing trees at least once a year. Not long ago he fell out when a branch gave way. Neither that nor my admonitions discourage him from tree climbing."

In other words, neither his wife, nor his publisher, nor angry subscribers and advertisers, are going to persuade editor/columnist Jim Smith from climbing out on limbs.

Because that's where you must occasionally go when one of your principal missions is to protect our First Amendment.

Bill Breisky has been a newspaper and magazine writer and editor since Dwight Eisenhower was our president. He has edited newspapers in Connecticut, New Hampshire and Massachusetts—most recently as editor of the Cape Cod Times *for 17 years—and resides in Sandwich, Massachusetts. Both he and Jim Smith were presented the Yankee Quill award from the Academy of New England Journalists. Smith's speech follows on the next page.*

The Yankee Quill speech:

Jim Smith won the New England Society of Newspaper Editors Yankee Quill Award in 2003 and, like the other recipients, he gave a speech at the awards dinner.

Smith was one of four journalists to receive the Yankee Quill Award that year. The others were Paul LaCamera, president and general manager of Channel 5, WCVB-TV, Boston; Stephen A. Kurkjian, senior assistant metropolitan editor at the Boston Globe, *and Harry T. Whitin, editor of* The Telegram & Gazette *in Worcester, Mass. Each was recognized by the New England Society of Newspaper Editors and the Society of Professional Journalists with the lifetime achievement award, given "for effort and dedication of those in New England who have had a broad influence for good in the field of journalism." Recipients become members of the Academy of New England Journalists.*

Former Pulitzer Prize board chairperson Geneva Overholser, who has has served as editor of The Des Moines Register, *ombudsman at the* Washington Post, *and a member of* The New York Times *editorial board, didn't hear the speech. But she read it and when she finished she wrote to Smith: "Oh, man. This is so wonderful. Your speech makes my heart stir. It should have wider distribution." So we put it in this book:*

IT IS NOT our job to sanitize the news

When I think of everything the *Record-Journal* has to cover—and ponder how I can persuade my publisher that we need more people—I think of my father, also Jim Smith, when he worked at a small weekly in upstate New York in the early 1950s called the *East Rochester Despatch*. He was reporter, editor, ad director, press foreman, and a few other things. When he was done reporting and writing and processing black-and-white film, he would build and draw ads—he was also the advertising artist (that is, after he sold the ads, because he was the ad sales staff, too). Then he would go to the composing room and sit down at the huge Linotype machine and set all the type. He took the pages to plate-making and made the plates. Then he put them on the press and cranked it up. He bundled the 2,000 copies of the *Despatch* and put them in the back seat of his Ford convertible and drove them to the post office. And then he started it all over again the next week.

I can see my publisher out there smiling. I should add that my father admitted the *Despatch* wasn't a very good paper, with its staff of virtually one, but it made a profit.

I have a few things I'd like to say tonight, the first of which is to thank my father for the molten lead and printer's ink in my veins, and my mother, a true poet, for showing me the value of putting one word after another on paper. They are no longer with us, but somebody I trust told me that in fact they are here in this room right now.

They knew Reid MacCluggage, who had a distinguished career at *The Hartford Courant* and *The Day* of New London and who received this award in 1995. Reid hired me for my first full-time reporting job 32 years ago. He has been a steady guide and an inspiration all these years and I thank him for that. Very early on I came back from a routine assignment and he asked how it went. I told him I asked all the usual questions. He looked at me for a moment and said, "Did you ask any unusual questions?" And then I knew, even routine assignments can make good stories if you ask the right questions.

Joel Rawson understands that. He is the executive editor of the *Providence Journal*, one of the finest newspapers in the country. He has been my good friend since college days and I thank him for his support of my nomination for this award.

Some of the things I have to say you may not agree with and, my God, we are in a room full of journalists—and though too many in the public think we are a monolithic power with a monolithic mindset, we all know that if you put a bunch of journalists in the same place at the same time, there is next to nothing we agree upon.

I'd like to say that capitalism is strangling journalism. I'd like to say that political correctness is running rampant in too many newsrooms across the land, with too many journalists too afraid of possibly offending a few readers. And I'd like to say that storytelling is an ancient and noble art that we all should be proud of.

The rock and the hard place: profit-seekers are the rock, readers are the hard place, and we are caught in between. To increase profits we steal from the readers. It began 25 years ago with the idea of no jumps—sound bites for readers. Legions of us believed that Americans were not deep enough to turn the page, could not digest more than six to eight inches on the largest issues facing them. Gannett staked its reputation on sound-bite journalism in print—the dumbing-down of journalism for dumbed-down readers. So that *USA Today* could succeed, it stole reporters from the company's other papers. Guess what? Those papers couldn't cover their communities as well. Guess what else—all those dumb readers figured it out and began saying, "Why read this rag?"

I will not bore you with the litany of disturbing budget cuts across the industry in the past decade. Newspapers have cut staffs, cut newshole, cut whole sections. The bean counters stand around and scratch their heads and wonder where have all the readers gone.

Here is one tiny example, though it is no small story to Kathy O'Connell. She was the features editor of the *Middletown Press*, a lively, family-owned daily on the Connecticut River. Kathy worked there for 18 years until the family sold out and it wound up in the hands of the Journal Register Co. of Trenton, N.J. Almost immediately employees were called into a back conference room one at a time and given the news by men in neat suits. They told Kathy that the paper no longer needed a features editor and did she have any questions.

"Just one," she said, rising from her chair: "How do you people sleep at night?" Oh, the *Middletown Press* has gone in a few short years from more than 20,000 daily circulation to about 10,000.

At the *Record-Journal* we have had some cutbacks, but nothing like what is going on in corporations like JRC. We hired Kathy

O'Connell and we hired other editors and reporters trying to get away from the suffocating management and shallow journalism of such companies.

A sharp publisher in the newspaper business knows that readers care about their community and if readers know the paper cares, too, they are going to care about the paper. The White family, the owners of the *Record-Journal*, cares deeply about the community it has served for more than a century.

Ah, readers. Should we offend them? Well, it can be an offensive world out there and it is our job to tell the truth about the world, the community, the neighborhood. It is *not* our job to sanitize the news. I ask you what happens to credibility if your job is to tell the truth—what happens to credibility every time you decide to leave truth out of a story?

Every time we decide to sanitize the message—water down the description, toss out the poignant quote, crop or toss aside the gripping photo—we sanitize truth, we whitewash reality, we censor the news. Tough stories need tough telling. We fail too, though, if all we do is tough stories. The world can be ugly, but the world can be beautiful. What happens to credibility when we ignore beauty, when we write only about failure when there is success to write about too?

A newspaper every day is filled with all kinds of stories and pictures. If someone complains about one story, tell them to turn the page; they'll find something they like. We need to stop apologizing for what we do. We need to exult in what we do. We need to remind readers about the sacredness in a free society of free speech and freedom of the press. We need to remember that storytelling is noble and remind our readers that writing builds civilization.

There are academic theories—see Walter Fisher's work on the narrative paradigm, for example. The former director of USC's Annenberg School of Communication, he holds that storytelling is what makes us human, that formulating and evaluating stories is how we reason, communicate, figure things out.

In ancient societies, before writing, those chosen to tell stories were revered. Prehistoric storytellers and balladeers could literally go on for days holding audiences enraptured because before man invented writing, we needed to hear stories. We discovered man's first written story in clay tablets in Mesopotamia. It is called "Gilgamesh."

It is a stirring tale about fighting evil, slaying dragons and—like Ulysses—having sex with goddesses. Nothing like sex and violence for a good story! There's a flood chapter with an ark—before the Bible came out! Gilgamesh is a story of friendship with lessons of right and wrong and it has come down to us over 5,000 years on clay tablets.

Do not cave in to those who are offended by writing. Remind people that writing is a basic human function and that writing news in a democracy—well, there couldn't be a democracy without unfettered news writing. Remind them we are publishing the first draft of history.

I wrote it this way a year ago:

"Life on this planet is troubling, exciting, uplifting, sad, happy, horrifying, beautiful. If a newspaper is supposed to reflect life and if you are reading a newspaper that does not portray horror, beauty, happiness, sadness, excitement or trouble—if it doesn't uplift you and make you laugh or make you cry—what kind of newspaper is that? It is an irrelevancy at your doorstep every morning. It is not worth your time. It is bland and blank and missing the parade of life as it goes by."

We can explain without being arrogant. We must insist on seeking the truth and we must find ways for American citizens to understand the importance of doing that.

Newsrooms are wonderful places. There is nothing like a newsroom. I fell in love in a newsroom and I married her. Jacky Smith edits my column, supervises our features department, handles our projects and general assignment reporters and writes her own column. Perhaps she doesn't have quite so many duties as her father-in-law had at the *East Rochester Despatch*, but like him, all the editors at the *Record-Journal* have a lot to do.

Over at that table there sit the top editors of one really good little newspaper in Connecticut. Dorothy Hall, Glenn Richter, Ken Robinson, Jacky Smith, Ralph Tomaselli; and the White family, Eliot and his sister Alison Muschinsky; our general manager, Mike Killian—we have worked side by side now for more than a decade. We have put out 4,190 *Record-Journals* together. Each day we try hard to do our best. And each day we say let's do it better. It is an honor to work with them. I am honored and humbled by this award and I surely thank the academy for seeing fit to give it to me. Thank you.

—James Smith

Acknowledgements

I WANT TO thank *Record-Journal* Assistant Managing Editor Glenn Richter for his nearly 14 years of meticulous editing of these columns. The opinions are mine, but when he suggested changes in usage or tone or grammar, he always made the writing better. I'm indebted to *Record-Journal* publisher, Eliot C. White, who encouraged me to write about the free press and how his newspaper gets out every day. The news staff of this great little newspaper calls it "the miracle on Crown Street." Reid MacCluggage, former managing editor of *The Hartford Courant*, was the first to encourage me to write opinion columns when he named me sports editor of *The Courant* in the early 1980s. My daughters, Barbara Ann, Sarah, Stephanie, and Rebecca, have always challenged and inspired me. I'm also indebted to the people and public officials of central Connecticut who read and reacted to these musings.

I hope, as I move a little further west to Bridgeport's *Connecticut Post*, that the readers and the movers and shakers are every bit as alive, vibrant, and vigilant as the folks in Meriden and environs have been.

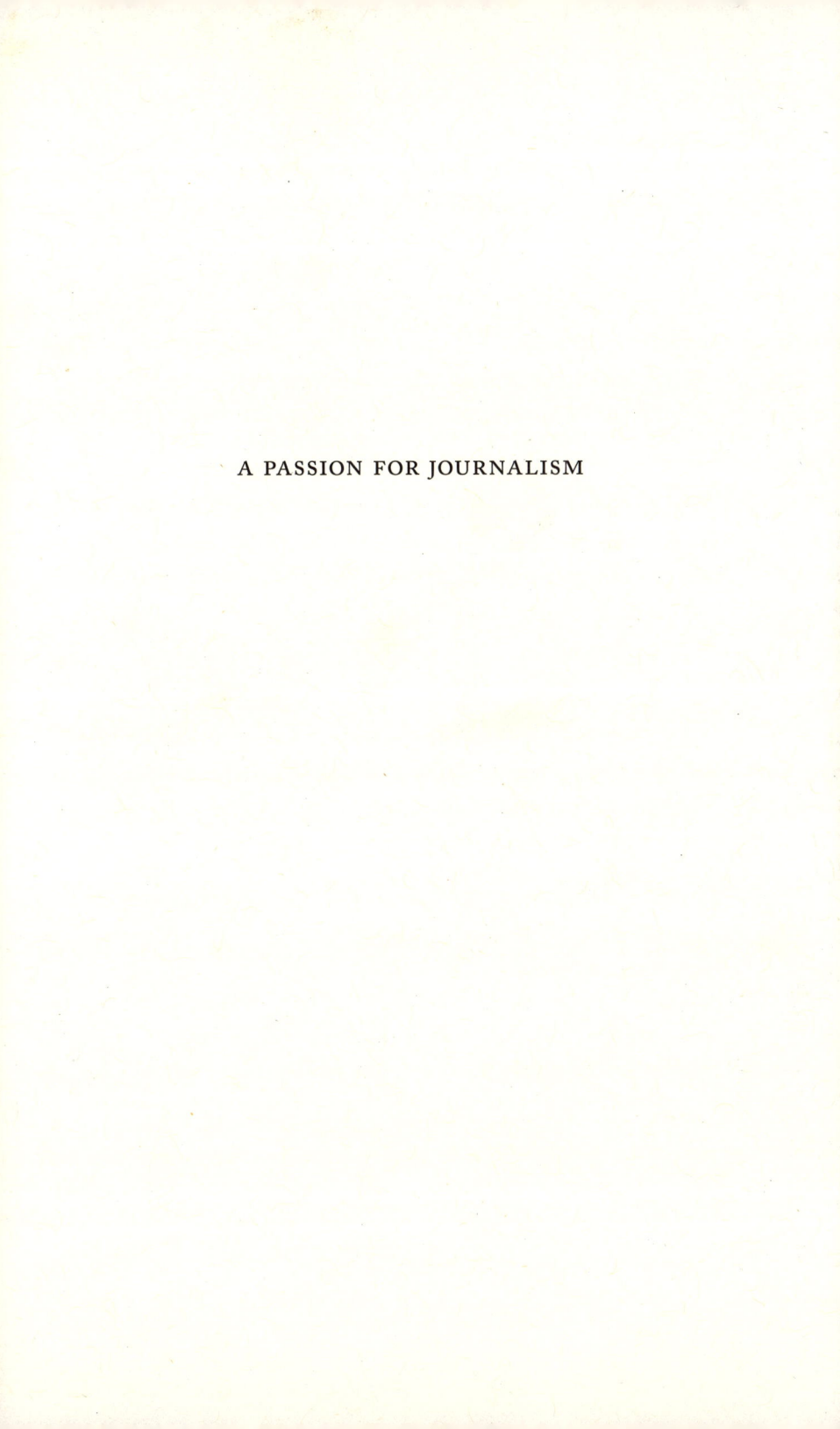

A PASSION FOR JOURNALISM

— 1994 to 1998 —

⁝ Messenger's plea: Don't shoot!

THE TURN-OF-THE-CENTURY ADAGE that a newspaper "comforts the afflicted, afflicts the comfortable" still holds true.

Finley Peter Dunne had been writing his columns for nine years when in 1902 his alter ego, Mr. Dooley, assured readers that "Th' newspaper does everything f'r us." For decades, readers loved Mr. Dooley and his populist philosophies.

A hundred years after Mr. Dooley was created, I take his "afflicts the comfortable" wisdom not necessarily literally, but more as a challenge to all of us in our increasingly comfortable lives to think beyond our own safe ideas.

As a society we too often dig in with our own entrenched thoughts, which is the path to intolerance and stagnation.

We in the media see this almost daily as viewers, and readers react to what is broadcast and published. The *Record-Journal*, like other newspapers in America, tries to publish what is real and true about the world, to include all shades of belief and opinion in our pages. This disturbs people because they encounter ideas and lifestyles different from their own. Their first reaction is to try to censor the publication, shoot the messenger. Here are a couple of examples, one more important than the other.

A woman named Cheryl called last week and told me our

Chief Photographer Chris French was a pervert for taking a picture of a woman in Wallingford selling hot dogs and wearing a bathing suit top and short blue-jean cutoffs. Too short for Cheryl, who began to judge the moral character of the woman in the photo.

In brief, Cheryl was intolerant.

She wasn't alone. Some women who work at the *Record-Journal* thought we were being sexist or gratuitous for printing the photograph. So did some men.

I see it as a slice of life and I cringe at censoring life.

Could the paper be accused of not truthfully reflecting life in greater Meriden that day if we chose not to print the picture? Perhaps not. But it was a scene around town that day, just as was the photo of the two little boys at their lemonade stand. I liked both photos, one certainly more provocative than the other, but beauty is in the eye of the beholder. What is lewd to one reader is pretty to another.

Let's up the ante a little with a story the media ran that upset many in our audience. When the former Hamden school superintendent was arrested on drunken driving charges while wearing a dress, many readers thought what the man was wearing is none of the public's business. Why would the press print that, they asked? It only hurt the poor man.

I think we need to ask ourselves how much truth should the press withhold from the public? If we didn't print that the man was wearing a dress, decided to leave that fact out, wouldn't readers wonder what other facts we leave out?

It is a matter of basic trust. If it is a newspaper's role in a democratic society to inform the public, to get as close to the truth as humanly possible, then we have to be careful not to chip away at the truth. That includes truth in words and photographs.

One of the great strengths of America is the diversity of its press.

How dull it would be if every news outlet were the same as the next. *Playboy* publishes full frontal nudity. The *Record-Jour-*

nal doesn't. In presenting the brutality in Rwanda, *Newsweek* has printed photos that *Record-Journal* editors felt were too gruesome.

Editors need to know their audience, not pander to it, and, in fact, to challenge it. We do not tell our photographers to find bland photos to bore our readers. We don't like to sanitize reality, but we know there are photos inappropriate for our readership. Within accepted standards of decency, what you have in the *Record-Journal* is an alert and aggressive news team bringing you life as we find it. Life is happy, sad, joyful, angry, frightening, frustrating, uplifting, and dull. We'll try to keep the dullness to a minimum in the pages of your local newspaper. Mr. Dooley would like that.

July 10, 1994

Private lives, and a public challenge

OK, IT'S A burgeoning issue, this phenomenon of the press writing about the private lives of public officials.

We didn't used to, we are reminded over and over. When the president of the United States was having bedroom liaisons with a Mafia girlfriend, we didn't write about it. And certainly our baseball heroes on the trains all those years were pristine pure because sportswriters never dreamed of printing the off-field "antics" of Babe Ruth and company.

Alas, the presidential hopes of Sen. Gary Hart were dashed by the *Miami Herald* when it printed that the candidate was spending the night and long weekends on exotic islands with a woman other than his wife.

Right here in Connecticut, a male school superintendent was

arrested for DWI while wearing women's clothes. Legislators were so outraged that TV and newspapers would make such a thing public of a public official, that they passed a law making it a crime for police to even mutter what an alleged criminal was wearing at the time of his or her arrest.

Then there was the recent secret getaway of the governor of Connecticut. Off he went and the public didn't know where he was. Journalists across the land are soul-searching and holding seminars and writing essays on just how much the public should know about our public men and women. It is an unending debate, I'm afraid.

Where oh where do we draw the line?

Well, let me tell you, it has been rumored around town that famous moderate Democrat Thomas S. Luby has been rolling his car windows down and playing his radio loudly. It hasn't hit the New York tabloids yet, so this is my own little scoop. Indeed, according to the utmost reliable sources, Mr. Luby actually embarrassed one of his three daughters while dropping her off at school and at the same time blaring "Wild Thing" out the window.

It could have been more than one daughter, but there is no question the former Connecticut House majority leader stated to his daughter that "Wild Thing" is his favorite song. He was probably even air-guitaring at the wheel to the strains of

Wild thing, you make my heart sing
You make everything groovy.

I, for one, always suspected that Mr. Luby was groovy. And I am not certain what effect this news will have on his status as the new president of the Democratic Leadership Council, the state chapter dedicated to supporting moderate and conservative Democrats.

He was only 14 when The Troggs released their only number-one single, described by *Rolling Stone* as "their five-million selling seminal punk hit." The song was so popular that it even spawned a parody performed by two people imitating Robert

Kennedy and Sen. Everett Dirksen, which is most likely Mr. Luby's favorite version.

The song enjoyed a revival a couple of years ago with the movie *Major League*, featuring Charlie Sheen as the "Wild Thing" pitcher. Maybe Mr. Luby and his daughters watched it together.

Now, no one ever said that columns had to be fair. But, heck, it could be argued that a newspaper editor or columnist is almost as much of a public figure as the president of the Democratic Leadership Council. So I will admit here, publicly, that last Wednesday in front of some 60 fifth-graders at Doolittle School, I air-guitared to "Wild Thing." I even sang a few lines and told them it was one of my favorite songs.

This was with no instrumental assistance, not even a radio to play along with. I simply, during a lesson on writing, succumbed to the spontaneity of classic rock.

So, Tom, do you remember the name of the Troggs' only other song to make the Top Ten?

April 2, 1995

Good fences make good newspapers

A TANNING SALON owner recently was incensed at a reporter who refused to give her more prominence in a story about tanning. "I advertise in your paper. I spend a lot of money in your paper," she insisted.

The reporter, as she has done many times, tried to explain to the businesswoman that there is a strict separation between advertising and news and that she would not receive preferential treatment because she is a *Record-Journal* advertiser.

Some advertisers get very upset at that and don't understand why. The tanning salon lady spent $3,000 on *Record-Journal* ads and that ought to count for something, she said. Other advertisers spend ten times, even a hundred times that amount and still it holds no sway with reporters and editors.

Here's why.

Newspapers "should not give favored news treatment to advertisers," states the Associated Press Managing Editors Code of Ethics. "Advertising should be clearly differentiated from news." The code couldn't be more clear.

Advertising is the major source of revenue for newspapers. Without it, most newspapers would go bankrupt. To have a free press in America, you must have a profitable press, one of my favorite former publishers was fond of saying. But he would never have dreamed of breaking journalism's ethics.

"The newspaper should report the news without regard for its own interests," according to the APME code.

At the *Record-Journal* we have more than 50 reporters, editors and photographers who work hard each day to bring our readers a fair, balanced and accurate account of what happened yesterday in the community, the nation, the world. At the same time, more than 30 hard-working and creative *Record-Journal* advertising men and women find good display space for advertisers, whose basic message is "our place, our product, our service, is the best." One pursuit doesn't hold higher ground over the other. News and advertising are, quite simply, different.

The contract with our advertisers is that an ad in the *Record-Journal* will bring more customers to your business. That is capitalism at work. It's a deal struck between our representative and the advertiser, be it a local tanning salon or Sears. The deal does not, can not, include a story. It's strictly business: Buy an ad, you'll make more money. Our Advertising Department serves our advertisers.

Our News Department serves our readers, no one else. "Freedom of the press belongs to the people," states the American Society of Newspaper Editors Statement of Principles. "The

First Amendment ... guarantees to the people through their press a constitutional right, and thereby places on newspaper people a particular responsibility.

"Thus journalism demands of its practitioners not only industry and knowledge but also the pursuit of a standard of integrity proportionate to the journalists' singular obligation."

ASNE defines that obligation like this: "The primary purpose of gathering and distributing news and opinion is to serve the general welfare by informing the people and enabling them to make judgments on the issues of the time. Newspapermen and women who abuse the power of their professional role for selfish motives or unworthy purposes are faithless to that public trust."

So, if we allowed advertisers to buy their way into the news columns, we would be saying that we are biased, that we do favor one person or one institution over another—"You want us to write about you, just fork over a little cash." We would be violating our public trust. If you aren't trusted or believed, who would read you? Just as we can't let our personal political beliefs get in the way of presenting the news, we can't let economic interests get in the way, either.

May 21, 1995

Chewin' the fat with Slats Grobnik

I FOUND SLATS GROBNIK with his head down over his beer at his usual downtown Chicago bar. I knew I couldn't cheer him up, but I tried. "Did you read how the *New York Times* said Mike had 'a tough skin and a generous heart?'" I said to Slats.

He looked up. "Yeah. Nobody can write obits like the *Times* obit writers, he said. I liked the part where they said Mike Royko's columns were 'as much a part of Chicago as the wind.'"

"And how about Mayor Daley saying the other day how Mike loved Chicago. Nobody went after Daley's father like Royko. His book *Boss* just stripped that guy naked," I said.

"You're tellin' me! Mrs. Daley, the present mayor's mother, got some supermarkets in town to ban Mike's book. But it wasn't his book, or even his Pulitzer that made him great," said Slats, "it was his columns. Five days a week, year after year, decade after decade. He was embarrassed when he cut back to four a few years ago.

"What did people in Connecticut think of him?"

"Well, sometimes they didn't get all the Chicago stuff. Sometimes they didn't understand that when he scolded politicians it was because he loved his city more than they did. But he wrote about everything, all the issues. I loved it when he called Jesse Jackson Jesse Jet-stream when Jackson was telling everyone to vote, but he flew out to California for a speech and, of course, couldn't get back to vote."

"That was a good one," said Slats. "Jackson said he'll never miss votin' again. And how about when he went after Reagan for hackin' away at programs for the poor but spendin' more on the military contractors. D'ya remember what he wrote?"

"Sure," Mike wrote "'Contrary to popular belief, it's much wiser to take money from the poor than the rich.' Even Jesse said Mike Royko was 'an equal opportunity shot taker.'"

"You bet he was! He hated bombast and self-important egomaniacs. One of his best lines, remember, was when he quit the *Sun-Times* when Murdoch bought it. Mike went over to the *Tribune*. He wouldn't work for Murdoch. Remember what he wrote—that no self-respecting fish would be wrapped in a Murdoch paper!" said Slats.

"That one made me laugh out, I love it when writers make you laugh," I told Slats, but he still was feeling low. Mike had been dead only a couple of days and Slats didn't know what to do.

He took a sip of his beer. "Ya know, Jim, not everybody knows this, but I'm not the first alter ego for a columnist in this town. There was a guy named Finley Peter Dunne who started writin' in 1892 for the old *Chicago Times*. Mike was only five when Dunne died in 1936. But Mike knew all about Mr. Dooley who was in Dunne's columns. It was Mr. Dooley who said 'The newspaper comforts the afflicted, afflicts the comfortable.' Now that was a good line, wished I'd said it."

"Listen, Slats. You and Mike said so many good things. You and Mike were the voice of the working stiff in this country. When he died, the AP said Mike used biting sarcasm—probably better than anyone—and that he had 'empathy for the common man.' That *Washington Post* critic, Howard Kurtz, ya know him, he wrote that book about what newspapers need to do to keep readers interested. He said, 'Turn writers loose.' And, Slats, he said this:

"When Mike Royko takes aim at a juicy target, it's the talk of the town. Newspapers need to keep people talking."

Slats knew his time was over and I could tell he was wondering who'd be the talk of the town.

May 4, 1997

⁞ Exercising judgment on these pages

WHEN THE POLITICAL debate ended the other night, after I had spent 60 minutes trying to keep track of who went first and who was speechifying past their allotted time, I wasn't prepared for the next encounters.

First, a dignified, well-dressed lady with a pretty smile told me she felt cheated out of a chance to ask a question. As moderator, I apologized.

But she was less concerned about debate procedures and wanted more to tell me how she disliked my column. Specifically the one about moving the war monuments from Broad Street.

"You shouldn't use the newspaper," she said, "to put out such a message."

Then a well-spoken man came up and questioned my wisdom over what stories we select for the front page, but more on that in a minute.

I was speechless for a moment about how I "use the newspaper." I pondered what she was saying in a pleasant, yet firm, voice. I played it back in my mind: "use the newspaper." That's my job, I was saying to myself. The *Record-Journal* pays me good money to write my opinion, and I should earn it by stating my opinion clearly in this space, I thought.

"Well," I said to her, "my column is my opinion. You don't have to agree with it."

She didn't. She almost harrumphed, and walked away before I could get her name.

She is not the only one to tell me I'm wrong about the monuments. I believe we should move them to a quieter place where we can contemplate the sacrifices of our fallen veterans in peace.

The power of the press can be mighty, but I hold no hope this particular idea will ever get past the words on this page. No one in this town would ever dream of moving the monuments. However, I do reserve the right to get my view across here. If you don't agree, that's fine. Signed columns give you the chance to think about something other than your own opinion.

I love laboring over a column because I love to write. I also love to edit, and that means putting my personal opinion aside.

Decisions about what goes on the front page, are based on news judgment, a thought process acquired through education, training, instinct, and experience.

The quiet, well-spoken man who pulled me aside is a parishioner at St. Stanislaus Church. He objected to our coverage of some disagreements between members and the parish priest. He especially wanted to know why we put on the front page a story about the priest and whom he selects to supervise the cheerleaders. It seemed to him a trivial tale.

His name is Dennis. I missed his last name. I told him he was probably right, the cheerleader story didn't belong on the front page. It was my decision and it was probably the wrong decision.

But I disagreed with Dennis about the larger story. He thought it was not much more than gossip. I thought it was a solid piece of reporting about fundamental differences between longtime parishioners and their priest, Father Ed Nadolny. The differences are so great that some have left the church or have been invited by him to pray elsewhere.

St. Stan's is a storied church in Meriden, with a long history and a large parish in a very Catholic town. We thought it was a story worth telling. The fellow standing before me didn't agree, but he allowed that it was a balanced account that showed both sides. Amen. Reporter Chris Gaither and his editor, Michael Kelley, did a fine job at producing an article with balance and depth.

Personally, I admire Father Ed and have since 1971. But there are people who don't admire him and said so in that article. Our readers are richer for having read it. And I'm glad we reported, wrote, edited, and published it.

October 26, 1997

⁞ Anthony's story needed to be told

"ANTHONY'S SILENT WORLD," written by Julie Fishman, photographed by Anna Leshchiner and edited by Michael Kelley and Jon Olson, has touched people's hearts like no other piece of journalism we have published this year.

The story of the 4-year-old deaf boy and his family living in a poor section of the city has horrified readers, prompted offers of everything from wall paint to furniture, elicited demands for action by appropriate state and local officials, and stirred friends and neighbors to defend the boy's mother and father. In the deluge of phone calls and letters that have poured into the newspaper, readers wanted to know why the *Record-Journal* published the story and photos. To many, it was disturbing. They want to understand the processes by which a newspaper tells such a tale.

Anthony Digres's story was published on the front page with a full page of pictures inside last Sunday. To me the story is disturbing, but it is also one of hope. There was peeling paint, cockroaches, too little food, an unkempt house and yard, and a husband and wife who are separated. But there was a father who admitted paying his debt to society with a prison term, who is working at a job and who visits his son every day. There is a single mother on welfare who is looking for a job and who makes sure her son attends the American School for the Deaf in West Hartford.

Ms. Leshchiner's photos are stark and gripping. The image of the young boy clad in only diapers climbing a shaky wooden fence barefoot just above a pile of garbage is a shocking portrait of life. Yet right next to that photo is another, a tender, touching, happy moment between father and son in their backyard.

Ms. Fishman's prose is poignant, descriptive: "Anthony lies in the tub half immersed in about three inches of water. The torn shower curtain hangs from a rusted, bent rod. . . . He crawls out of the tub and stands shivering. His mother is in the neighbor's apartment upstairs. Anthony pulls a dirty wool sweater over his wet body."

Ms. Fishman and Ms. Leshchiner spent a lot of time with this family. They went over with the parents how the story and photos would portray their life as it is. They let the parents explain their situation. Amy Digres says she knows her son should not be left alone in the tub but "he tells me to leave. He washes himself. He likes to lie down. It is his little quiet time."

Readers ask did we do this to prompt government action, or to find donations for the family. The answer may sound too simple: We published the story because it was there, because it is real. Often newspapers will print articles in an effort to change conditions, or at least make the public aware that something needs reform. It is called a "news hook." But some stories don't need hooks. Some stories just are.

It is our job to publish stories and photos. That is our chosen profession and we believe newspapering serves a high purpose in society. Julie Fishman holds a master's degree in journalism from Columbia University. Anna Leshchiner studied photojournalism at Syracuse University as did her editor, Jon Olson. Michael Kelley, Ms. Fishman's editor, is an honors history scholar from the University of Connecticut. He also is a husband and a father.

These people not only know and love their craft, they have families too. It is not just our training and education that helps us try to understand the human condition and to portray it in the pages of this newspaper. We go about our work with as much sensitivity, courage, fairness, and an unending pursuit of the truth as we can muster day in and day out. Anthony's story is disturbing. Anyone who has read it, including his parents, are that much wiser for having done so.

November 30, 1997

⁞ Let the story continue

I WAS WITH Geno all the way, up until he decided to bash the press. That's the way it always seems to go. Public people who choose a public life always get around to blaming the press.

"You guys just want a freakin' story," Coach Auriemma said Thursday, after the entire civilized world couldn't stop talking about Nykesha Sales' famous gift of an unopposed lay-up against Villanova Tuesday, giving her UConn's all-time women's scoring record.

When you're in the writing game, yes, you want a story. God help civilization if the stories ever stop. In the scheme of things, what's more important—writing stories or playing basketball?

Our "guy" on the UConn basketball beat is a woman, Terese Karmel. In one of her freakin' stories she wrote that Geno Auriemma "has a soft spot deep within him, a still place in the churning figure, and it is reserved for just a few of his players— past and present. . . . Sales seems to have staked the most special claim on her coach's heart more than any previous player."

That observation is as beautiful as any of Kesha's graceful assaults on a hoop 10 feet high. The thought behind those sentences is as profound as any of the coach's strategies on the hard court.

Isn't it fascinating how we have lifted sport to such importance in our lives? Fishermen in Gloucester are talking of the shot. Ladies making pierogis in church kitchens are talking of the shot. Cosmonauts on the Mir are no doubt debating the ethics of competition.

Shouldn't we remind ourselves it is just a game? This isn't hunger and starvation, truth and lies, war and peace. This is a basketball game, for goodness' sakes.

OK, there was a time in my life that nothing was more important than basketball. The Friday night meal had to be just so much, cooked just right, in preparation for the big game. I was the shortest guy on the starting five, but, by God, I was on the starting five! We made it to the playoffs and when we lost in the quarterfinals, I cried. I was 17. Alas, my basketball career was over.

When you're in the game, it has meaning. But watching? Why such a fuss about giving away two points, getting them back, then starting the competition from scratch?

In my years as a varsity coach, when each season wound to a close, I made sure the seniors played. Even though some under-classmen were better, and they gave us a better chance to win, seniors always started the last game. It was their last chance to play. I don't remember whether we won or lost those games, but I remember they played—and I'll bet they remember. The game is for them, isn't it?

How about in the Mick's final year of his career when he stepped to the plate and a young and brash Denny McClain grooved one down the middle for him? Mantle says to the catcher—did he mean that? Yep. Next pitch is coming fast and down the middle, Mick. A gift. He dings it for number 534 or maybe 535, edging to his final 536 home runs. Any aster-isks around Mantle's numbers? Anyone worried about Mantle's competitive edge?

Who can say what is more important? Is it the dancer, the singer, the painter, the doctor, the architect, the plumber, the writer or the athlete who contributes more to society? Picasso, Pavarotti, Hemingway or Jordan?

You want a shot to remember? To date in UConn history, it is the one at the buzzer in 1990: "The basketball left Tate George's fingers in a high arc, accepting the instructions of his hand with stunning obedience. Swish."

Just as the player was performing under pressure, my writer at the time, Tommy George, wrote that account to meet a buzzer of his own, the deadline to press start. Mr. Tommy George's sentence is as memorable as Mr. Tate George's basket. Let the games go on, let the story continue.

March 1, 1998

⧟ Should I even ask the question?

I FOUND MYSELF at lunch the other day with three women who work in local government. The conversation drifted to sex in the Oval Office. If Monica Lewinsky offered it, and then pleased the president of the United States with oral sex, should we all know that? I wondered out loud.

One woman leaned forward, looked me right in the eye, smiled, then said sternly and with conviction: "You shouldn't even ask the question." The other two women didn't hesitate to nod in agreement. Even if it happened in the Oval Office, it is nobody's business, they insisted.

Several years ago, rumors spread through Meriden that a certain woman in city government offered and gave the same favor to the mayor at the time in his office. A janitor supposedly popped in on them.

The *Record-Journal* never printed that story. It was only hearsay. The mayor didn't have a federal grand jury after him. Not a single soul was alleging that he was trying to obstruct justice by having the local lady lie about it.

We all know the president of the United States has said he didn't have sex with Ms. Lewinsky, then a White House intern. If he's lying and persuaded her to lie to the special prosecutor and the grand jury, he is encouraging perjury. That is a crime, and, according to some in Congress, an impeachable crime.

Kenneth Starr, the special prosecutor, disagrees in no uncertain terms with the women at my lunch table. He is asking the question of just about anyone he can pull in front of his grand jury, including the intern's mother. He would love to indict the president of the United States, if not for a bad real estate deal 25 years ago in Arkansas, then for his escapades in the Oval Office.

It's not really the sex that Mr. Starr is interested in. It's the lies. He can't indict the president of the United States for extramarital sexual activities. He can't even indict him for lying. He can get him for, as they say in legalese, suborning perjury—getting the lady to lie for him.

I try to stop and think once in a while at the curiosity level of the people. Probably Mr. Starr wouldn't want my lunch mates on his staff. They don't want to know from nothin'.

I probably wouldn't want them on my staff either, nice and intelligent as they seemed. When we hire reporters, we look for a certain level of curiosity. Reporters need to find things out. Like police and prosecutors, they need to know how to ask questions. Unlike police and prosecutors, who put people in front of judges, reporters put it in the newspaper. They write about it. They write about what prosecutors and police and judges and presidents do.

I joined these ladies at lunch after a morning of listening to 1) experts on the state Freedom of Information laws; 2) experts in the collective bargaining process and union grievance procedures. Most of the 150 people in attendance thought collective bargaining should be done in secret. The unions don't want the public to know their demands—"What if we were asking for orthodontist coverage in health benefits?" asked the union rep. Right, what if? Surely management doesn't want to appear stingy on orthodontics.

Don't even ask the question!

Hmmmm, I say to myself. Why shouldn't we know if we're going to pay for orthodontics?

If Monica Lewinsky had been wearing braces . . . never mind.

If Ms. Lewinsky and the president of the United States were not exactly conducting presidential business together, should we know about it? If the mayor of Meriden and a City Hall colleague were otherwise engaged in the mayor's office, should we know about it?

Most Americans, like the women lunching with me, say no. I'm not convinced. I like asking questions and finding answers.

April 5, 1998

School board delivers a wise verdict

WHEN YOU'RE AT a book-banning meeting, things get a little scary. You listen to people who say they don't want to start a bonfire, who say they aren't talking about censorship, and who do not understand the very words they are speaking.

They wanted *Deliverance* out of Sheehan High School and as they paraded to the microphone one by one last night—holding up the Bible, quoting Scripture, speaking of Judeo-Christian values—they insisted one of the greatest poets of the century was degrading our teen-agers. If you believe in open minds and the pursuit of knowledge and free inquiry in the classroom, you begin to worry that the book-banners just might prevail.

But the parade of Sheehan seniors was longer. Some weren't as polished in their presentations, a few freaked out and couldn't quite finish their message. If there was an enduring image in the school auditorium, however, it was student after student after student getting up and saying thank you, thank you, thank you for James Dickey and his novel and please, please, please don't take it away from the seniors who will come after us.

When was the last time you saw high school kids show up en masse to defend their homework assignments? As the book-burners decried the degeneration of societal and family values, it was as if they missed all the 17- and 18-year-olds stating as clearly as they could, "Let me learn, let me read, don't take this away from me." I lost count of how many, but these were not seniors out cruising and boozing last night. They were high school seniors at a school board meeting, composing a significant portion of the audience, defending their teachers for teaching them James Dickey's novel.

And they won.

Their teachers talked of owls and Christ symbolism in the modern classic. A "memorable and important book," according to English teacher and football coach Dennis Mannion. His colleague Patricia Juliano told the school board members who would decide the fate of the book that the main character dreamed of soaring with an owl and "overcame his metaphorical blindness."

Owls can signify wisdom, and Dickey uses owl imagery to foreshadow important passages in the book, said Mannion. "I tell my students to pay attention to the significance of events when owls appear in this novel," he told an attentive board and audience of some 200.

An intense Charles Rinaldi, his jaw set hard under his salt-and-pepper beard, staked his nearly 30 years of teaching English on the "extremely well written" novel. He shuddered at the "specter raised by the very attempt to ban a book in a democratic society" and condemned the effort as an abridgment of the right to think what we choose.

School Superintendent Joseph Cirasuolo asked again and again in a litany of literary masterpieces: because one person may object to one passage, "does that mean that none of our students can read it?" Because Romeo and Juliet have premarital sex, and if one person objects, "does that mean none of our students can read it?"

Dennis and Eileen Allard, who brought the complaint, handed out a sheet "to adults only" of passages they object to, including this they consider derogatory to women: "I kept looking for a decent ass and spotted one in a beige skirt...."

At the end of three hours of testimony, the board voted 7-1 that such sentences aren't enough to ban the book from the 12th-grade reading list. If parents object to it, their son or daughter can be assigned a different book. That's a fair policy, said board Chairwoman Patricia Corsetti.

Dickey's daughter Bronywn, a 17-year-old Choate student, spoke in defense of her late father's work. After the vote, she went over and hugged the Sheehan teachers.

May 1, 1998

21

⁞ The truth isn't always pretty

NEWSPAPER PEOPLE HAVE always felt the wrath of readers who tire of the unending parade of "negative" news delivered to their door each morning, bringing yet again terrorists, scandals, corruption, killings, fires, death, destruction, governmental bungling, burglaries, rapes and shootings, in words and pictures.

Journalists wring their hands over how to inform an educated public. A whole lot of editors in the land of the free are throwing up their arms, dumbing down their news stories and censoring their photography. These editors think that if we upset our readers too much, they'll stop reading. They could be right, but I think they're wrong.

The free press in this free country is held responsible for writing and photographing the truth. If we say it is our job to print the truth, what happens every time we decide to leave things out, present only part of what we know to be true? You start to lose trust. Why trust purveyors of half-truths? If you aren't trusted, aren't believed, who will read you?

Newspaper people shouldn't ask, "How much truth should we tell today?" We shouldn't sanitize life. Presenting the raw truth might offend some readers who prefer a sanitized version. But I believe intelligent readers want their world presented in real terms, or as close to reality as we can get.

James Joyce, trying to publish *Dubliners*, his first collection of short stories, faced a publisher who asked him to "suppress" certain passages because "an inconveniently large section of the general public" will object.

Joyce rejoined, "I cannot alter what I have written. All the objections ... arose in my mind when I was writing the book. ... Had I listened to them I would not have written the book. I have come to the conclusion that I cannot write without offending people." His book was finally published and he is recognized as one of the greatest writers of this century.

Murder and mayhem are messy. Funerals are sad. Corruption is disgusting. All of it can be offensive. Should we try to portray all this as it is, or soften it into what it is not?

We should take care to cover the world and the community in all of its glory. Wholeness—all sides, not just both sides—is a concept of coverage this newspaper endorses. Hold a mirror up to your community in the pages of your newspaper and make sure the image you shine back is whole and true. Over time, intelligent readers know whether you are giving the whole picture.

The *Record-Journal* news staff met not long ago to talk about how we cover our community. We revised our decade-old guidelines. Here are some of them:

"Truth, accuracy and fairness are the hallmarks of good journalism. To get there, use the time-tested formula of who, what, when, where, why and how. Some coverage will be offensive to some readers because the subject of the coverage itself is offensive. . . . Writing about, or taking pictures of, a tragedy will, by definition, be a tragic telling of the event. We would be unfaithful to our profession, our very purpose, by doing less than the best we can to tell . . . what happened.

"Our responsibility is to the facts, the truth or as close as we can get to it. Our news judgments need to incorporate the fact that the *Record-Journal* is a family newspaper with children as readers, and so we recognize some parameters. We do not, for example, identify the victims of sexual assault. . . .

"Readers get incensed at what they see as the insensitivity of the media. This is answered best, not by diluting tough subjects, but by making sure our coverage is whole—that we cover success as well as failure, what is beautiful as well as what is ugly, what uplifts as well as what disturbs."

June 13, 1998

⁝ What kind of pledge is that?

THOMAS JEFFERSON DIED on the Fourth of July, 1826. Precisely 50 years earlier he and a few other revolutionaries created the Fourth of July by signing a little document Jefferson had penned deriding a certain despot named George III and declaring that "We hold these truths to be self-evident, that all men are created equal, that they are endowed by their Creator with certain unalienable rights, that among these are life, liberty and the pursuit of happiness."

Before I raised our American flag in the yard this weekend, I looked up Jefferson's letter to Madison, the one written after we beat the British but before we adopted our Constitution.

The author of the Declaration of Independence wrote to his friend in 1787 that the Constitution looks pretty good except for "the omission of a bill of rights—what the people are entitled to against every government on earth . . . and what no just government should refuse." Jefferson, then ambassador to France, urged Madison to make sure our new government provided "clearly for freedom of religion, freedom of the press . . . trials by jury" and our other basic rights. Madison did.[†]

I was reminded of all this sitting at lunch recently with 19-year-old Tisha Byars and her parents. The quiet, polite, pretty young woman had just finished her freshman year at the University of Connecticut and was about to receive the Deane C. Avery Award. *The Day* of New London awards it annually to an individual who advances the cause of freedom of information or freedom of speech.

This year the award stirred some controversy, as did her fight against the Waterbury school system. An honors student, she wasn't invited into the National Honor Society because, school officials said, she ate corn chips in class and was rude to a teacher. Ms. Byars and her parents thought differently. They said school

---

[†] The Bill of Rights is printed at the back of this book on page 153.

officials barred her because she refused to pledge allegiance to the flag.

A federal judge ordered the school to induct her into the honor society, as he should have. Further, the court ordered the school district to put in writing that students cannot be forced to pledge the flag.

Jefferson and Madison resolved this with the First Amendment's guarantee of free speech, which also guarantees the freedom NOT to speak. The U.S. Supreme Court resolved it again on Flag Day, 1943, in the middle of World War II. It ruled that a school system can't force a Jehovah's Witness to pledge allegiance.

It is Tojo and Hitler who forced their people to pledge allegiance to their flag. Great democracies don't need to coerce loyalty. The Bill of Rights "guards the individual's right to speak his own mind" but West Virginia was trying to compel a student "to utter what is not in his mind," said the Court. "To believe that patriotism will not flourish if patriotic ceremonies are voluntary and spontaneous instead of a compulsory routine is to make an unflattering estimate of the appeal of our institutions to free minds," Justice Robert H. Jackson wrote for the Court.

The students refused to salute the flag because it would violate their faith, which forbids worshipping an image. Ms. Byars, who is African-American, refused to pledge the flag in Waterbury because she does not believe there is "liberty and justice for all."

I don't know if Deane Avery agrees with her on that. He is the retired editor and co-publisher of *The Day*. I do know he believes strongly in free speech. He flew fighter planes off aircraft carriers in World War II, landing one so shot up and crippled it had to be shoved overboard.

He sat at our lunch table with dignity and a smile as Ms. Byars accepted the award. He applauded as she quietly said thank you.

July 5, 1998

— 1999 —

Rights are forgotten in Meriden

WALTER CRONKITE SAID two decades ago that "Freedom of the press is not just important to democracy, it is democracy." Oprah Winfrey put it this way last year: "Free speech not only lives, it rocks!"

Not, however, in the minds of Meriden school administrators and members of the Board of Education. The board just adopted a punitive new policy without devoting so much as a brain cell—not one expressed thought—on the importance of our Bill of Rights. It was a disturbing sight to behold, astonishing that some of the most educated people in this community can completely ignore the basic values of this democracy established at the very founding of our government more than 200 years ago.

The 1999 policy states that they can expel students for "threatening in any manner, including orally or in writing, harm to the person or damage to the property of a member of the school community, including any teacher, member of the school administration, any other employee, or a fellow student."

Their intent is to keep the schools safe. Schools need to be safe so that students can learn. But in a free society, even in a controlled environment such as schools—and I would argue especially in our schools—we believe we are not safe unless we protect basic human rights. That's why Oprah proclaims that free speech rocks.

But it doesn't in Meriden with this mindless policy change. It is a threat to democracy. As they sat there discussing the wording at their first meeting of the new year, they placed a comma between "writing" and "harm." A comma is not enough. The gulf between saying something or writing something and actually doing something, is the historic boundary that protects free speech, yet the leading educators in this city never gave it a second thought.

Now if someone overhears a student say, "If he touches my girlfriend once more, I'm going to break his nose," they can expel him from school—even if he says it in his driveway. Or let's say a sportswriter for the school paper, in his exuberance for a football victory, writes that "the Panthers should kick and stomp a bloody path to every touchdown over the Trojans," they could expel him for "threatening in any manner."

If our local educators had cared to make even a cursory check of First Amendment history, they would have found Justice Oliver Wendell Holmes' 1919 famous decision popularly known as "clear and present danger." He wrote: if "the words used are in such a nature as to create a clear and present danger that they will bring about substantive evils," the person uttering them can be punished. Fearing he was blunting free speech too much, he altered the ruling later that year to not just "danger" but "imminent danger."

In 1927 Justice Louis Brandeis modified it further by declaring: "In order to support a finding of clear and present danger, it must be shown that immediate serious violence was to be expected." By 1941 the court moved to protect free speech even more, by ruling that the result of threatening speech must be "extremely serious," and "the degree of imminence" very high. Finally in 1969, the Supreme Court decided that the "clear and present danger doctrine should have no place in interpretation of the First Amendment." In other words, threatening language is part of free speech.

The freedom to speak and write is fundamental to life in this country and ought to be one of the most important concepts that we teach our students. Instead, the Meriden school board has established rules that teach our students just the opposite. What is more frightening is that they did this without uttering one thought about the Bill of Rights.

January 17, 1999

Choices: What's in a word?

WE SPEND A lot of time discussing what words, what messages to put in these pages. We do it from the standpoint of an unalterable commitment to free speech and free press, which, as we all learned in school, is writ into the U.S. Constitution as the First Amendment.

This week we wrestled with whether to include the words "sexy-assed mastodon" in today's edition. We know that children read the *Record-Journal*. And we know that a Southington High School history teacher was disciplined for allowing those words in a student magazine. The phrase was part of a satirical piece of writing by an anonymous student that included a pretty good description of French kissing, the outing of a man who dresses as a woman, and a brilliant, deep, and insightful ending: "The sun continued to shine that day."

Southington High Principal Jerome Auclair didn't find that story appropriate for the student writers' club publication. I think he's wrong, but I understand that educators try to find the proper balance for what is permitted in the schools. Just as we try to determine what is proper to put in this newspaper.

I don't think, for example, we ever spelled out the F-word. We do print some profanities, but not others, and we always consider the context—whether they are essential to the truth of the event or issue being covered, or whether the words are merely gratuitous.

You may have found already, I'm sure, today's front-page articles by Eric Cotton and Mary Milewski examining the status of free speech in our schools. As local school boards and school administrators tighten down on what students can say and write, we wanted to look at the issue in a broad context. We present experts and professionals of long experience in both education and constitutional law, and articulate students who choose to write.

Some of what is being discussed is how school boards are clamping down on students in the frightening wake of school-yard murders in the Midwest. Teachers are afraid.

My fear is that we cannot let fear erode our liberties. That is the trail to totalitarianism. I go back to the men we trust, the men who created our form of government. I find Benjamin Franklin, as early as 1759, writing, "They that give up essential liberty to obtain a little temporary safety deserve neither liberty nor safety."

His thoughts make me wonder about teachers accepting money from students. The infamous Jed Molaver, now in college, who wrote in parody about putting a pistol to the head of one of his teachers, needed an editor, not a prosecutor. His punishment includes not only an apology to those teachers, but payments of up to $2,000. I ask, what kind of teacher accepts $2,000 from a student? What kind of teacher prompts a student, a good student, to be so frustrated as to write such comments?

We need to ask what are we teaching our students about basic American rights. The Meriden school board adopted a new policy that allows students to be expelled for what they say.

That policy was adopted without even a public reference to free speech, and raises serious concerns about the school district's commitment to the teaching of the Bill of Rights.

Children, students, even high school students old enough to vote and serve in the armed forces, do not enjoy the rights of adults. But if their teachers don't teach them about rights and if principals punish students with no regard for basic rights, what do they learn? They learn that it's OK to take away rights.

I don't think we want to teach that and it should trouble all of us that educators are so easily heading in that direction.

John F. Kennedy put it this way: "Liberty without learning is always in peril and learning without liberty is always in vain."

January 31, 1999

Finding what is true is highest calling

I HEARD THE speaker say, "Truth is not the most important entity in society." It gave me pause. It made me wonder if I heard him right. What could be more important than truth?

The Bible tells us the truth shall set us free. Chaucer told us "Trouthe is the hyest thyng that men may kepe." Gandhi said there is "no god higher than truth." Jefferson reminded us that we are not "afraid to follow truth wherever it may lead"; and in his most famous writing, "We hold these truths to be self evident."

But this fellow would have none of that. From where I was sitting, he was sort of a sourpuss. He didn't smile. He is New York lawyer Martin London, billed on the program as a legal expert who "often jousts with the press."

Here he was at the University of Connecticut School of Law

grumbling loudly that it is "simply outrageous that the press can violate your privacy just to get to the truth."

The truth is, I knew I wouldn't like him before I even got there. But he made me think beyond the subject of the discussion about things that may be more important than truth. Mr. London thinks privacy is more important and also the lawyer/client privilege, as in "it is preposterous that a newspaper reporter could intrude on the lawyer-client privilege."

It reminded me of the time Frank McDonald, who probably will become chief justice of the state Supreme Court later this year, put me on the witness stand to force me to tell the truth in order to get around the lawyer/client privilege. As a state prosecutor he put me on the stand, made me swear to tell the truth, the whole truth and nothing but the truth about a murder case I was covering. Specifically he asked, when I was lunching with the suspect and his lawyer, did I hear the man confess to the crime.

No, Mr. McDonald, I did not hear that. If I had heard that, you would have read that in my newspaper, I testified under oath.

Now, maybe the murderer (he was convicted) did tell his lawyer he stabbed two people to death, but of course a good defense lawyer would never say that. Lawyers aren't always interested in the truth. Privilege and privacy are more important to some.

Before all my lawyer friends toss this page in the birdcage, I understand it is important to defend your client; in fact, it is in the Bill of Rights. And because we have such smart lawyers and judges, the truth does not always win in a courtroom. Just ask O.J.'s lawyers.

So maybe the right to a fair trial is more important than truth.

But then, no less a man than Nobel laureate Linus Pauling believed that science "is the search for truth." So is journalism, yet we journalists and scientists know the search can go on for a long time. Science has yet to tell us how old the universe is and journalism hasn't yet fathomed who's making out financially in the Wallingford open space deals.

Come to think of it, truth isn't high priority to a certain number of public officials.

Consider Keats, who felt truth was beauty and imagination. You can find truth in almost all of his poems.

As for me, love can be more important than truth, and sometimes love must hide. But at its best, it is called true love.

Truth hides too. It is elusive but it is there. We lose our way if we think it doesn't matter. Like equality, one of Jefferson's self-evident truths, it is one of the basic foundations of a just society. We cannot lean on a foundation of lies. Thinking becomes a sham if it is based on falsehoods.

Keats is part right. Truth can be beauty. But it can also be ugly. In the seeking, beauty is its own reward, but we shouldn't shrink when we know the trail leads elsewhere.

Finding what is true is the highest calling.

May 30, 1999

Let's salute for the right reasons

WE ARE SALUTING the flag this weekend because Flag Day is tomorrow. As we contemplate Old Glory, we shouldn't bow to blind patriotism, and the ceremonies shouldn't focus solely on the military.

America is much more than our military. Blind patriotism turns too easily to closed minds. America is about open minds.

All nations have flags and have comparable celebrations about the glories of their nation, symbolized by their flag. Serbs love their flag. We don't, and they don't love ours.

When we raise the Stars and Stripes, we think about why we love our country. Compared to Serbia, the United States hasn't been around all that long, but we've learned lessons faster than they do in the Balkans.

If we pinpoint our beginnings at Jamestown in 1607, we are nearly 400 years old. That's roughly half the age of the glory that was Rome. Perhaps we will have learned enough so that what we love and believe in will last longer than the Roman Empire. Maybe we can bring places like Serbia out of the darkness.

We were once there. We were guilty of ethnic cleansing. Just ask a Sioux or an Apache. We massacred, murdered, ethnically cleansed—whatever you want to call it—American Indians with very little remorse. Then we pushed them out of their country so we could have it. We said things like "The only good Injun is a dead Injun."

We don't anymore. Serbs do. We have learned from our mistakes. Serbs haven't. I don't mean to pick on just the Serbs. Inhumanity to man can be laid at just about everyone's feet: the Germans, the Japanese, the Russians, the Chinese, the British, the Italians—almost everyone.

We taught the Brits a lesson 1776–1783, and then again for good measure in 1812–1814. We didn't like their monarchial repression so we kicked their butt. They didn't learn. A mere 30 years later they starved half the Irish in a genocide they did not apologize for until just a couple of years ago. Even our most enlightened societies—they did give the world Shakespeare—are guilty of heinous crimes.

We are proud of beating the British. I'm not sure how proud we should be of beating the Mexicans or the Indians, or the Cubans and the Filipinos; and don't forget the Grenadians. Hey, but we won. We can be proud of defeating the Germans, the Austro-Hungarians, the Italians, the Japanese, and the Confederates. We made the world safe for democracy and we stopped beasts like Hitler and Mussolini. So salute the flag and remember our soldiers who paid dearly for beating them.

But don't stop there. Love our flag and our country because we now know it is wrong to commit genocide. We now know it is wrong to enslave human beings.

A Serb may not want to live next-door to an Albanian, but at least a lot of Americans don't mind living next-door to a Pequot or an Apache or a Hispanic or a black family. Right? The glory of America is the opportunity and justice and equality. It is other places where they don't let you read the news because they don't let the news out.

As you salute the flag consider the greatness of this country in its literature, from Thoreau to Angelou, and remember that you can read them whenever you want to. Consider Remington and Warhol, Gershwin and Dylan. You can view their masterpieces and listen to their music any time you want.

We have not erased hate and intolerance, or eliminated censorship, but we have condemned them. From Roosevelt to Reagan, from left to right, we praise America, we pledge the flag, because of its promise. And it is a promise we have kept better than anyone else.

June 13, 1999

Freedom of (or from) religion

HAPPY FOURTH OF July, our 223rd. July 4, 1775, was just another day. July 4, 1776—oh my!

The signing of a document by 57 men—revolutionaries ready to hang for their signatures—from 13 colonies, changed the world.

The very "laws of nature" and "nature's God" wrote Thomas Jefferson, entitled Americans to declare their independence because "all men are created equal, that they are endowed, by their

Creator, with certain unalienable rights" including (all together now): "life, liberty and the pursuit of happiness."

England's King George III didn't quite agree and waged war for six long years until Lord Cornwallis surrendered to George Washington in 1781.

I thought we might take a moment today and reflect on one of the unalienable rights: our freedom of religion. There seems to be such confusion of late, what with Congress thinking it's a good idea to put the Ten Commandants in public schools and a profusion of angry letters to the editor about how there are too many laws keeping prayers out of the schools.

In England and most of the rest of the world in the late 18th century, you had to practice a particular religion in order to hold office or own property. If you believed differently than the approved religion, you were an outcast.

The American Revolution changed all that. Mr. Jefferson was the prime motivator for religious liberty.

He started even as the war raged, before we knew we might win. In 1779 Jefferson wrote his "Bill for Establishing Religious Freedom in Virginia." He began by stating that "Almighty God hath created the mind free." He went on about how leaders, both civil and religious, had endeavored to impose on others their own beliefs "through all time."

"To compel a man to furnish contributions of money for the propagation of opinions which he disbelieves, is sinful and tyrannical," he penned, and "our civil rights have no dependence on our religious opinions." The Virginia Assembly passed the bill stating "no man shall be compelled to frequent or support any religious worship . . . nor shall otherwise suffer on account of his religious opinions or belief." It declared that if any acts are passed to narrow religious freedom, "such act will be an infringement of natural right." It was new thought, that human rights were part of the natural law of things.

Later the new United States of America institutionalized Jefferson's ideas in the First Amendment to the Constitution:

"Congress shall make no law respecting an establishment of religion, or prohibiting the free exercise therof." The Constitution set up the Supreme Court to make sure Congress didn't go astray, as politicians tend to do. Our founders knew that way back when.

There you have a very brief recital on why we shouldn't be required to pray in public schools, which are part of the government. Decades of Supreme Court decisions have given us a road map on religious liberty. In a landmark 1947 case, the court ruled: "The 'establishment of religion' clause of the First Amendment means at least this: Neither a state nor the Federal Government can set up a church. Neither can pass laws that aid one religion, aid all religions, or prefer one religion over another."

Schools have been battlegrounds because of the captive audience aspect in a classroom. It is hard not to pray if you choose not to, when everyone is told it's time to pray. What we believe, dating back 223 years, is that praying is personal and no one can tell us when to or when not to.

This does not prohibit the study of religions in public schools, comparing the beliefs of Christianity with Islam and Judaism and Buddhism and the rest. That is an appropriate enterprise in education.

July 4, 1999

Should news be run by the government?

IT WAS ANOTHER one of those bad days. *Editor & Publisher*, the magazine that covers the newspaper industry, reported two weeks ago about yet another study showing the public losing confidence in the press.

This latest survey of 1,001 adults (done by UConn's Center for Survey Research and Analysis) reveals that 53 percent think the press has too much power, and more people who believe the government should stop the press from printing news. Two years ago 80 percent of adults believed the press should be free to publish without governmental approval. That number is now down to 65 percent.

To me, that is startling and un-American. It makes me wonder if our schools are teaching our basic beliefs. Do we learn about the Bill of Rights anymore? From the very beginnings of our republic, the press was designed to be a watchdog on government, free from control by government. It is dictatorships, not democracies, that control newspapers.

If so many Americans truly believe this, how do we get back to understanding the role of the press in a free society? One First Amendment expert, Paul McMasters of the Freedom Forum near Washington, D.C., said of the survey results, there has been "a steady alienation on the part of the public from a press that they see as too pervasive, too sensational, too superficial . . . too biased and . . . getting things wrong."

One at a time for now—Is the press too pervasive?

Ever since scribes first etched figures in clay, someone has been on the scene to record what happened. For nearly two centuries, journalists have been reporting news each day and have always been criticized. Newspaper reporters and editors were supreme until about 35 years ago, when television news caught up, and the practice of journalism became more visible—more pervasive.

Very few people *saw* print reporters ask questions. Often they are tough questions asked of officials and others in the news who don't want to cooperate. It has always been hard to gather the news because there are so many people who don't want it to get out. To be a good reporter and get the information we believe the public has a right to know, oftentimes you must be aggressive.

In the television era with news crews carrying cameras and microphones, the public now sees the news-gathering process and it is not always pretty. In fact, some of the best broadcast journalists raised the interview to a high art. Think of Mike Wallace on *60 Minutes*, or Barbara Walters' incredulous facial expressions at Monica Lewinsky's answers.

Think of Columbine High School or Baghdad. You never know what will happen as CNN rolls the cameras live. Good or bad, instantaneous communication is here to stay. It *is* pervasive and news gathering is the lightning rod. We cannot get away from knowing instantly that bombs are falling on Iraqis or Serbs, or children are shooting each other in school.

This new technology lays down new responsibilities on reporters and editors. Think of the moment when a student inside Columbine High School couldn't reach the police on his cell phone so he called the local television station. On live audio, the boy was about to say where he was hiding when the alert anchorwoman interrupted and told him not to reveal his location.

In the newspaper business we still have a full day to sift information, make editing decisions, and try to bring some sense and context to what is happening.

How do you feel about news? Should the government control it? Is it too pervasive? Let us know. We'll try to answer your comments and questions.

July 25, 1999

Everybody's got at least one opinion

A COUPLE OF weeks ago, I asked readers if they thought the press was too pervasive and if the government should control the media. A new poll showed that one third of adults believe the government should control what is printed or broadcast and that the credibility of the press is eroding.

The responses were thoughtful and to the point. "I disagree with most of your" columns and found this latest one about the press "comical," wrote Bob Swick of Wallingford. He wondered why he reads the "misinformed, liberalistic, biased views of our community" he finds in the paper.

Two other Wallingford readers abhorred the idea of censorship. "Government definitely should not control the press," wrote Joyce F. Kowalczyk.

"It's disturbing to think of how many people believe it would be OK to erode the ability of the press to observe or investigate the operations of our government, our so-called political leaders or some of our corporations and their leaders. Does anyone believe they always have the best interests of our country or 'The People' in mind?" wrote Mike Camarata.

Ms. Kowalczyk found fault in the "minute-by-minute coverage TV gives everything they consider 'breaking' news to keep you on their channel. Whatever it is, Monica, Diana, Kennedy . . . it is non-stop. I watch the news for what is happening in the *rest* of the country and world as well, and often have to endure repetitious pictures (remember Monica being hugged by President Clinton?) and comment."

She and Mr. Camarata worried about corporate conglomerates taking over news outlets. "The press is often just another big business with profits more in mind than its role as society's watchdog," he said.

Retired journalist Bob Greene, whose first reporting job was at the old *Morning Record*, blamed slipping credibility on sloppy writing. "The dumbing down of the educational system has produced ignorant people who, sadly, don't realize they are ignorant. They have no context and their grammar and usage is often poor to abysmal . . . They often don't know how to organize their thoughts to clearly express themselves, which is essential in good writing. The art of writing a crisp, clear lead (first paragraph) to a story seems to be a lost art." Now there's a man who understands that clear writing comes from clear thinking.

But back to Mr. Swick. "I see no balance in presenting of facts. Articles by Mr. Sambides, editorials by Mr. Smith, Powell and Collins lambaste anything that does not fit into their very narrow view of supreme liberalism, they are all basically right and everyone else is wrong (and we) are forced to read this biased journalism which exhibits the writer's own failed liberal views. Yes, Mr. Smith, your press especially is too pervasive. Objectivity is non-existent in your world."

He points up a confusing fact about journalism. Reporters write balanced articles, columnists don't. Mr. Sambides' coverage of Wallingford Town Hall is fair and balanced. It has to be—that is his job. I have no idea what his personal political beliefs are. We balance columnists by publishing many different ones. My column, and Bill Collins's and Ron Powell's are more or less liberal, while Chris Powell, William Safire, Cal Thomas and Glenn Richter are more or less conservative, to name a few.

Some criticism comes from conservatives opposed to liberal views and vice versa. But a great strength of newspapers is that we print opinions of all stripes. "I don't always agree, but I'm pleased to read Glenn Richter, Ted Moynihan, Mike Roberts, Ron Powell, Ralph Tomaselli" and others, said Ms. Kowalczyk.

I'm pleased to hear from her and the others. Contact us anytime.

August 15, 1999

— 2000 —

White guys in suits are not enough

THE AMERICAN SOCIETY of Newspaper Editors can be a pretty stuffy crowd, a bunch of white guys in suits with their ties rammed stiffly against their necks. When Barbara and Carter White, the retired editor and publisher of this newspaper, attended the annual conventions, Mrs. White was somewhat of a pioneer. Very few women were editors in those not-so-long-ago days.

It is changing. Dozens of women are now editors. The immediate past president of ASNE is Sandra Mims Rowe, editor of the Portland Oregonian. Women rising through the ranks have had a profound effect on newspapers, giving them a wider view than when they were controlled only by white men.

What hasn't changed so dramatically is the sea of white faces in American journalism. The industry does not have a good record of diversifying its work force. Though it is more committed to change than many industries, newspapers can do better and must. The press, whose job it is to reflect society back to itself, to cover all of society not just white society—as it has been guilty of in the past—needs a diverse work force in order to fully understand a diverse society.

41

The *Record-Journal* has known this for years. News department management is committed to the idea that white men, no matter how open-minded, cannot make fully informed news judgments in a world where they make up such a small segment of the population. Our recruitment, hiring, training and promotion policies are designed to give equal opportunity for all. We don't wait for women and minorities to find us. We communicate with colleges, raid the competition (which is great fun), and attend job fairs. Our most successful program is the *Record-Journal* minority internship/scholarship, which we instituted in 1993, a year after I arrived here.

We send applications to local high schools seeking African-American, Latino, Asian-American and Native American students who are interested in a career in journalism. Applicants write a personal essay and face tough competition for the internships, which provide full-time summer work and a scholarship through four years of college. The package is worth $5,000 a year and has proved rewarding for the newspaper and students from Maloney, Platt, Wilcox Tech, Southington and Lyman Hall high schools to date.

Our two present minority interns—Deanna Chaparro, a young Latino woman who graduated from Platt and is studying at Central Connecticut State University; and Dan Champagne, of Native American ancestry, who graduated from Lyman Hall and is studying at Marist College—are both good enough already to be full-time reporters here. But they know it is best to get that bachelor's degree. We will help them do that and when they graduate we expect them to come aboard full time for their first newspaper jobs. One of our best copy editors, Ratnanjali Beniwal (Maloney High and Southern Connecticut State University), whose parents emigrated from India, is a graduate of our internship/scholarship program. Hiring people of diverse backgrounds enriches the workplace and makes the newspaper better.

We fully endorse ASNE's mission statement on diversity: "To

cover communities fully, to carry out their role in a democracy, and to succeed in the marketplace, the nation's newsrooms must reflect the racial diversity of American society ... At a minimum, all newspapers should employ journalists of color and every newspaper should reflect the diversity of its community."

According to ASNE, in 1978 there were 1,700 minorities at work in the newsrooms of America's daily newspapers out of a work force of 43,000, or 4 percent. Today, 6,365 minorities out of 55,100 journalists, or 11.5 percent, are at work. Not enough. But we are on the right path.

January 23, 2000

No hatred, no venom, just reality

IN THE 2000 version of the controversy over Wallingford's failure to observe Martin Luther King's holiday, I have been called many things. My logic is "convoluted"; I spew "hatred and venom"; I am "presumptive, sanctimonious, arrogant" and "breathtakingly stupid"; a "hypocrite" and—my personal favorite—my writing is "one big Blah, Blah, Blah."

These observations were contained in letters to the editor from readers who disagree with my view that Mayor William W. Dickinson Jr. is wrong to turn this into an economic issue, when it is fundamentally a moral issue.

As for this arrogant, stupid hypocrite, who should resign, said one letter writer, if the paper doesn't take King Day off, allow me an observation: criticizing the newspaper is an attempt to deflect the focus from where it should be—on the man who runs Wallingford. The critics would have a point if every other newspaper in the state took the day off and the *Record-Jour-*

nal did not. Of course, that is not the case. I don't want to be convoluted here, but I believe readers can grasp that 1) private businesses are far more stingy with days off than government is; and 2) there's a difference between a newspaper following general newspaper practice and a town government that is the only town government failing to follow federal, state and municipal holiday practices.

Lest we forget, newsrooms never close. We are staffed 365 days a year. We honor heroes like Dr. King by writing about them.

In the 12 columns I have written in the past year about Dr. King's holiday I find fault with the mayor and other local leaders. Contrary to the fellow who claims I spew "hatred and venom at Wallingford," I have not criticized the people of Wallingford, except in one narrow instance.

That was when some at a Town Council meeting blamed "outside agitators." I reminded them in writing what Dr. King wrote: "I am cognizant of the interrelatedness of all communities and states. I cannot sit idly by in Atlanta and not be concerned about what happens in Birmingham. Injustice anywhere is a threat to justice everywhere. We are caught in an inescapable network of mutuality, tied in a single garment of destiny ... Never again can we afford to live with the narrow, provincial 'outside agitator' idea. Anyone who lives inside the United States can never be considered an outsider anywhere in this country."

Connecticut towns are famously independent. Truth be told, Wallingford can tend to be more insular than other towns, even Southington, where they try to keep non-residents out of their parks. Our towns love being the masters of their destiny. Trouble is, they're not. They're not islands unto themselves. In our system of government, we are not citizens of towns. We are citizens of the United States.

I agree with Gov. Rowland that most of the people of Wallingford want to honor Dr. King like everyone else does and be rid of this stigma that is damaging their reputation. It is their local leaders who need to catch up with them. Democratic councilors finally proposed mediation, but the obstructionist mayor refuses. He is turning townspeople against town workers.

His figure on the "cost" of the holiday is $32,000 for overtime, or some 78 cents per person. That isn't worth one minute of controversy, much less 14 years. Some in the fray are stretching the truth, claiming that every other town swapped a holiday for King Day. We report today that most municipalities added the holiday.

With 40 letters to the editor and 30 articles and columns on King Day this year, the R-J is providing thorough coverage and a public forum for a community to talk to itself. Unfettered discussion will one day bring forth the answer.

February 6, 2000

If there's no freedom of the press, then there's no freedom at all.

WE COVER A lot of high school and middle school essay contests and even reprint in full the winning essays with pictures of the winning students. I remember one well-written piece in particular from a Holy Trinity School student in Wallingford.

He wrote that a football star he admired was also a minister who espoused family values. The young student criticized the media for criticizing his hero, Green Bay Packers defensive end Reggie White. It was an award-winning essay, but I took the time to share with the eighth-grader how if it weren't for the media he wouldn't know about the football star or his ministerial views.

It is television, radio, newspapers, sporting magazines and now the Internet that bring the games and the players to any who care. Unless you live somewhere near a major-league city and go to the games, the only way you will know about them is through some form of media.

It puzzles me when fans bash the sporting press, which brings them what they want: athletes to admire, or at least games to watch.

Of course, some athletes are not admirable and deserve criticism for failures both on and off the field of play. I believe "the minister of defense," as Mr. White is called, was disparaging gay people. Some in the media—talk show hosts like Dr. Laura or Rush Limbaugh, for example—would join in the disparaging. Others, like me, wouldn't and would find fault with the player/minister's intolerant expositions.

I hope we haven't gotten to the point in this country where we would try to censor the media, inclusive of men like Mr. Limbaugh. Should we stop baseball writers from assessing the value of a slugger who no longer slugs or a pitcher who can't find the strike zone? And if athletes venture into other endeavors where their actions or comments can be controversial, are we saying the scribes and commentators are supposed to look the other way, ignore it?

What is the value of a writer to society? As much as an NBA player? Less? More? I still hope that chronicling sports is as important to us as the games themselves.

And what about chronicling—covering, as we say in the news business—more serious pursuits in life like government, religion, education, science, literature, the arts, business, parenting, war, peace, human rights and on and on. In short, the parade of humanity as we move through time.

The parade passes right here and this local newspaper does

its utter best to bring it, in all its luster, glory, and ferment to thousands of readers each day.

All kinds of people try to stop us from reporting all kinds of things all the time. But it is our job to bring you the news, bad, good, and in-between.

Bad or good often depends on your point of view. We'd be in trouble if we empowered someone to start deciding they can stop the presses because they don't like the message.

During the Martin Luther King Day controversy, when we wrote a long profile of state Rep. Mary Mushinsky, the Democrat who sponsored legislation to force Wallingford to honor the holiday, Republicans howled that we were glorifying Mrs. Mushinsky, wasting ink on a woman who should be run out of town. How dare we give her such exposure in our newspaper? they said.

Then when we wrote an even longer profile of Mayor William Dickinson, the Republican who has fought to keep government open on MLK Day, Democrats howled that we were glorifying Mr. Dickinson, wasting ink on a man who ought to be driven from office. How dare we give him such exposure in our newspaper? they said.

What we did was to provide readers with a more comprehensive look at those two major protagonists in this unending drama than any publication ever has. And we are glad we did. And I am glad nobody had the power to stop us.

Often influential people in the community will try to pressure the newspaper to suppress stories they don't like. If we started listening to everyone who tried to keep things out of the paper, it would be a mighty thin publication every day. And we would be violating our public trust to inform the people of the things they need to know.

Here are three stories from this summer that three powerful, or at least influential, individuals involved in those stories tried to keep out of print, tried to keep the public from knowing about. When we went ahead with the articles, two of these people, at least to some degree, refused to speak on the record about the issue at hand.

Each is instructive, though not unusual for us. As I said, people ask, tell, demand all the time that we not print the news.

Meriden School Superintendent Beth Ruocco didn't want us to write about her contract provision that gives her children health benefits for life. Cuno Corp. Chief Financial Officer Frederick Flynn didn't want us to write about layoffs. St. Andrew's Episcopal Church Pastor Robert Broesler asked us not to write about the parish's problems with an alleged burglar.

The Rev. Broesler, whom I know as an enlightened, sensitive and intelligent man, was initially angered that we would even consider a story and insisted that it was a private matter to be kept within his parish. Furthermore, the experience caused deep soul-searching for many at the church, including himself. Over the objections of some church members, he embraced a stranger and tried to help the man get back on his feet only to discover that many valuable items began to disappear during the man's stay. The stranger was eventually arrested for burglaries downtown.

This was a heart-rending story about a very public minister and his traditionally very high-profile downtown congregation that deserved a full airing in the local paper, I suggested to him. In the end the Rev. Broesler sat down with a reporter and discussed what happened, including the moving account of his own emotional trauma.

His articulation of the tale in his own words made for one of the more memorable stories in Meriden this year, rife with lessons for anyone who read it.

Mr. Flynn was angered that we would write about layoffs at Cuno, especially in view of the fact that we had botched a piece about his firm in our annual business and industry review, which we had. Furthermore, he said, raising questions about layoffs could jeopardize the company's chances to get a state grant for employee training.

He was not happy with my response that the union was concerned about the possibility of more layoffs and that we don't kill articles because one side on an issue objects to its publication. I also pointed out that we had written about layoffs at our own company.

There is no question that Cuno is not only a major corporation in town but also a large benefactor to many worthy causes. So is the *Record-Journal*. Cuno makes filtration systems, a benefit to society. The *Record-Journal* makes newspapers, at least an equal benefit to society. We agreed to disagree on this one. Both firms will be here for a long time to come.

The Beth Ruocco story has a twist. A school superintendent's contract is news, especially such a lucrative one with that unusual provision for her family. The initial story caused a large controversy. There were things for reporters to pursue. Her supporters said her salary was in line with other superintendents and nowhere near the pay of a CEO of a private firm with revenues equal to the school budget. We found both to be true.

But why the lifelong health benefits for her grown children? Dr. Ruocco was adamant that that is none of the public's business. I begged to differ; the public would be paying for the benefit.

She did not like all this attention but understood that as the highest-paid public official in the city she is accountable to the public. But she refused to comment about her children.

We learned that one requires medical treatment and we learned for what. Dr. Ruocco argued forcefully that the medical condition was a private matter; she was the public official, not her offspring.

As editors we grappled with this. Where is the line of privacy drawn? Put a bunch of editors in one room and don't ever expect unanimous agreement. This case was no exception. Some argued that the public has a right to know why they were paying hundreds of thousands of dollars for an official's family.

In the end, I decided it was enough to publish that there is a medical condition requiring treatment. The nature of that medical condition is a private matter. We left it out of our coverage.

What is important to journalists and ought to be important to the American public is that it is a journalistic decision; that in a free society, the press must be free to write or broadcast.

Elsewhere kings or dictators decide what the public will know. In a democracy, journalists make those decisions.

September 3, 2000

You can't stop the chronicling of humanity, Senator.

AND YOU SHOULDN'T try to.

When I'm not doing journalism—nonfiction writing and editing—I dabble in fiction. One story I'm writing is set in the American Revolution when Gen. Washington sent an army against the Iroquois Indians in New York State.

There's violence in my story. Musket balls smash into foreheads. Indians slash the throats of Continental soldiers. There's scalping on both sides. A mean and vicious bluecoat attempts to rape a beautiful young Iroquois woman. It is a repulsive scene. Rape is repulsive.

I don't want Joe Lieberman telling me I can't write the story the way I want to. And I don't want him telling publishers that they can't market my story to teen-agers. Along with the violence—revolutions happen to be violent—my story has a message or two that young people should read.

Maybe a 10-year-old shouldn't, but I think that is up to the parents of 10-year-olds. It shouldn't be up to the U.S. Senate or the Federal Trade Commission.

51

Steven Spielberg made a graphic, violent movie starring Tom Hanks called *Saving Private Ryan*. Mr. Spielberg wouldn't let his 15-year-old son watch it. It was about D-Day and had many important messages and is a wonderful story. It is fine by me if the man who created it tells his son he has to wait a couple of years before he can see it. That's parenthood.

And it is good that the government couldn't stop Mr. Spielberg from making the movie.

But Sen. Lieberman is at it again—not to prevent violent videos from being made, but to pass a law "to give the FTC the authority under their false and deceptive advertising rules to bring actions against companies that continue to market adult-rated products to children."

I've known the good senator for nearly three decades. He is a good man; a bit of a warmonger, but a good man. On this issue, though, he is getting dangerously close to censorship.

He doesn't like the video game "Soldier of Fortune," where blood and body parts fly across the screen. Maybe video games aren't literature or even comparable to a good movie. But my fear is that when you start legislating against art or videos, or writing that you don't like them, where do you stop? And who gets to choose?

Storytellers have been around since the beginning of man. Before we could write, we told stories. For centuries, what we now call Epic Poetry was recited out loud by poets who held large audiences spellbound for hours at a time. They used suspense and voice inflection and conflict. Today we recognize these tales as some of the greatest literature ever written.

It is replete with violence.

We can read today man's oldest recorded epic, titled *Gilgamesh*. It came out of Mesopotamia more than 4,000 years ago.

Then Enkidu jumped out and seized the Bull of Heaven by its horns. The Bull spewed his spittle in front of him, with his thick tail he flung his dung behind him. . . .

Enkidu grasped it by the thick of its tail and held onto it with both his hands, while Gilgamesh, like an expert butcher, boldly and surely approached the Bull of Heaven. Between the nape, and the horns, and he thrust his sword. After they had killed the Bull of Heaven, they ripped out its heart. . . .

When Enkidu heard this pronouncement of the goddess Ishtar, he wrenched off the Bull's hindquarter and flung it in her face: "If I could only get at you, I would do the same to you! I would drape his innards over your arms!"

Jump ahead more than a thousand years to Homer and his *Odyssey*.

Odysseus took aim, and smote him with an arrow in the throat, and clean out through the tender neck passed the point; he sank to one side, and the cup fell from his hand as he was smitten, and straightway up through his nostrils there came a thick jet of the blood of man; and quickly he thrust the table from him with a kick of his foot, and spilled all the food on the floor, and the bread and roast flesh were befouled.

And Grendel's approach to a castle of sleeping noblemen in *Beowulf* has been called one of the scariest scenes in English literature.

Then from the moorland, by misty crags, with God's wrath laden, Grendel came. The monster was minded of mankind now sundry to seize in the stately house . . . the portal opened, though with forged bolts fast, when his fists had struck it, and baleful he burst in his blatant rage . . . He spied in the hall the hero-band, kin and clansmen clustered asleep, hardy liegemen. Then laughed his heart; for the monster was minded, ere morn should dawn, savage, to sever the soul of each, life from body, since lusty banquet waited his will! . . . Not that the monster was minded to pause! Straightway he seized a sleeping warrior for the first, and tore him fiercely asunder, the bone-frame bit, drank blood in streams, swallowed him piecemeal: swiftly thus the lifeless corpse was clear devoured, even feet and hands.

Pretty tough stuff.

Let's make sure teen-agers don't read it. They might try to shoot an arrow through someone's neck. For God's sakes make sure some video company doesn't get an idea of portraying Grendel chomping up some unfortunate knight, feet and hands included.

Sen. Lieberman and some colleagues have been trying their hardest for years to keep fake violence away from kids. They think it makes kids violent. They think if they see it in a movie or on TV or in a video or hear it in a song, then the kids will copy it.

They line up "experts" to overstate their case.

More than 1,000 studies "point overwhelmingly to a causal connection between media violence and aggressive behavior in some children," according to a statement issued last year by the American Medical Association and three other medical groups.

The trouble is, it's not true. In fact, a spokesman for the AMA later conceded that members of its board had not read any of the studies they were citing.

Psychology Professor Jonathan Freedman has read those studies and finds the medical consortium's statement "irresponsible."

Prof. Freedman, of the University of Toronto, has studied the research on media violence and says bluntly, "The scientific evidence does not support" what the AMA claims.

Some studies suggest a causal link between entertainment violence and violent acts in children, but "the majority of them do not. Normally, in science, you expect to get consistent results. It's irresponsible for any scientist to say that given the distribution of (these) results, this is proven," he told the Freedom Forum last July.

This kind of political propaganda leads us astray in tending to the needs of our children. In any segment of the population there are violent individuals who need help. We need to identify the real causes of violent behavior. Putting the blame where it doesn't belong won't solve the problem.

When I was a kid, my friends and I watched endless hours of westerns and World War II movies where more Indians, Germans, and Japanese were butchered than you could count. None of us went out afterward and started shooting.

Storytelling is too important to the human condition to let politicians try to quash it. All of them from Caesar to Stalin have tried. But it never lasts. Writers and artists will keep creating literature and art. Storytelling will never stop. Those who try through threats, through legislation, through book burnings are trying to stop the chronicling of humanity.

You can't stop it.

January 28, 2001

B.C. (before comic) there was the Constitution

A JOB APPLICANT came in for an interview last Monday and brought up a good point. Like all applicants worth hiring, he had done some homework and said he couldn't help noticing in the previous day's paper our coverage of the controversy over the "B.C." comic strip.

People from all over were calling it anti-Semitic and demanding that newspapers not print it. The young man applying for the reporting job said he noticed that I held it was a First Amendment issue and that is why we printed the strip; and that Editorial Page Editor Allan Church held it was *not* a First Amendment issue and that he would not have published the offending comic.

The applicant, a student at Columbia University Graduate School of Journalism, thought that it was good that editors on the same newspaper could disagree so publicly.

So do I.

And that is one answer, in case you were wondering why two senior editors could explain things in such different terms. In contrast to the stereotypical monolithic media filled with people who all think the same way, great debates ensue among journalists at every newspaper. Employing people with different opinions makes the American press more vigorous. Put a bunch of editors in a room—which we do formally twice every day—and there will never be full agreement, even on the First Amendment, which protects Americans' rights to freedom of speech, press, religion, peaceable assembly, and to petition the government if you don't like what it is doing.

Johnny Hart's comic strip depicted candles being snuffed out in a menorah, which transformed into a cross. I see its promulgation as a free speech and press issue. My colleague Allan Church doesn't. U.S. Supreme Court justices and the lawyers who have argued in front of them have disagreed over the First Amendment, so it is not really surprising two newspaper editors have a disagreement.

For the record, of course, I'm right and he's wrong.

Allan can speak for himself. And he did in his column last Sunday. "There is no First Amendment right involved," he wrote. "Johnny Hart has no First Amendment right to be published in this paper."

That's true. As some have acknowledged over the years, freedom of the press means freedom for those who own one. There's a man in northern California who owns one and publishes a weekly newspaper. But he has a problem. He won't allow anything in his paper that in any way supports abortion.

Someone should take his press away from him. Oops, someone should send him to First Amendment school. He is doing a disservice to his community.

Back here in central Connecticut, our editorial page editor acknowledged that if the government tried to prevent us from printing the comic strip, it would violate our right to freedom of the press. He also wrote that "no one is presuming to tell this newspaper or any other that we *cannot* publish the offending Hart strip."

Now we get into some gray areas. I heard from readers who said they would cancel their subscriptions if we printed the comic. Seven local clergy men and women, some of whom I know and respect, came close to telling us not to publish it. "We urge you not to run B.C. this Sunday as a matter of principle," they said in a letter to the editor. These are reasonable people doing their best to fight against what they interpret as religious bigotry.

But I wouldn't and didn't accommodate them, and here is why.

Because "The ultimate good desired is better reached by free trade in ideas, that the best test of truth is the power of the thought to get itself accepted in the competition of the market. That, at any rate, is the theory of our Constitution," wrote Supreme Court Justice Oliver Wendell Holmes in 1919. "We should be eternally vigilant against attempts to check the expression of opinions that we loathe and believe to be fraught with death."

Amen.

Newspapers are the place for Holmes' marketplace of ideas. Truth emerges from a full discussion. If we removed the reason for this discussion—Mr. Hart's cartoon—then how could the public fully participate or make a judgment? The cartoon is open to interpretation. The cartoonist himself said it has nothing to do with hate, but is a celebration of both Judaism and Christianity. Maybe, maybe not, but how can anyone make a decision if they can't see and read it? Why would anyone allow a clergyman or anyone else to decide for them that the thing is offensive. Offensiveness is in the eyes of the beholder.

If anyone is under an obligation to print what some see as offensive, it is a newspaper. To me it is the weekly publisher in California who is offensive. In censoring news about abortion, he doesn't grasp the hallowed meaning of free expression. As Justice Louis Brandeis reaffirmed in 1927, it is the "freedom to think as you will and to speak as you think."

Newspapers, as much as judges, must be in the vanguard of protecting the U.S. Constitution and its First Amendment against threats, even well-meaning threats. Journalists instinctively fight censorship, even if the newspaper institutionally disagrees with the point of view being expressed. It was only a few years ago in Wallingford that some wanted to ban the book *Deliverance* from the high schools. Whether you think James Dickey's novel was literature or trash, you harm fundamental American principles by supporting efforts to suppress it.

We have been besieged with pleas to ignore Matt Hale, the white supremacist who came to Wallingford yesterday for the second time in two months. He is a hate monger. You don't defeat hate by ignoring it—then it just festers. You defeat hate by exposing it—opening it to debate so that truth will prevail and all will eventually see how hate and prejudice are wrong.

If a proper role of a newspaper is to defend free expression, then it would be succumbing to the forces of censorship by banning a thought, or a photo, a song, a poem, a painting, or a cartoon, from its pages simply because there is a clamoring to do so. Yes, a newspaper has the right to print or not print what it chooses, and we make choices every day. It is when something is the specific target of attempts at repression that I will opt for publication because I believe that truth will emerge through a full and unfettered debate.

If you think Mr. Hart's cartoon is religious hatred, if you think Mr. Hale is hatred personified, I say put them out there so the people can see and judge them for what they are.

April 21, 2001

He raises a good question

ONE OF THE more fertile minds downtown belongs to Bruce Miller, who runs the YMCA, carries that lighthearted hint of a smile, and isn't afraid to think big. After all, he brought Meriden its most impressive new downtown edifice.

The Y is fun and so is Mr. Miller. But it is his serious side, his committed core, his toughness, that brought the city that wonderful building on West Main Street. And he'd be the first to say it wasn't just him.

But he has a little street fighter in him and gave us a jab not so long ago. It's not that those of us who labor in this much older building on the other side of downtown don't deserve a little jab now and then. Besides, the Y director was responding to a wordsmith criticizing his grandiose downtown arts plan.

Associate Editor Michael Kelley questioned whether a new playhouse and music hall with a $34 million price tag isn't a little rich for the city. So did some in the arts community, but then who could possibly bring together potters, painters, sculptors, thespians, cellists and singers to speak in one voice?

Mr. Miller jabbed that we at the paper "are artists, too; you paint powerful pictures with words. There is one thing that I have never understood. The *Record-Journal* is the largest downtown business, yet its employees consistently decline active participation, citing a 'conflict of interest' clause, as if somehow working to better your environs conflicts with reporting news."

We need some gray-area paint here. Journalists fervently believe we better our environs by writing about them. The very act of covering a community serves it as much as participating in it.

"The primary purpose of gathering and distributing news and opinion is to serve the general welfare by informing the people and enabling them to make judgments on the issues of the time," states the American Society of Newspaper Editors "Statement of Principles."

That requires "an independent scrutiny" and avoiding "any conflict of interest," according to the principles. The Society of Professional Journalists Code of Ethics requires us to "be free of obligation to any interest other than the public's right to know."

In 1996 a third group, the Associated Press Managing Editors, softened the prohibition of direct participation with this: "Journalists are encouraged to be involved in their communities" but only if "such activities do not create conflicts of interest."

The question for us is, can a reporter or editor join an arts committee that proposes to fundamentally change the nature of downtown without raising questions about the newspaper's impartiality? We take such questions seriously. However, it is not a science. We declined membership in Mr. Miller's group, but one of our editors volunteered to serve on the board that is refurbishing the Curtis Memorial. The difference is scale—the rebirth of only one building—and so we are comfortable with serving.

I'm on the steering committee of the Meriden Democracy Project, which sponsors study circles on race relations. Encouraging communication is the same mission of the newspaper and poses no conflict.

Newspaper employees who do not work in the news and editorial departments aren't bound by the same strictures. These ethics codes apply only to journalism. Many more people at newspapers work outside the newsroom in other departments. For example, our Marketing Director Sandra Blodgett serves as president of the United Way of Meriden and Wallingford; Senior VP for Sales and Marketing Michael F. Killian is a former president of the Southington Chamber of Commerce; and Publisher Eliot C. White has served on more community boards than we can count.

We thank Mr. Miller for raising a good question. We try to answer good questions.

May 27, 2001

Sometimes editing a newspaper is like walking a tightrope

AT A DINNER party recently the man sitting next to me said that the front-page stories in the *New York Times* are biased in favor of liberal views. A few weeks later a fellow I had just met insisted that all the *Washington Post* stories "are slanted in favor of Democrats."

It seems that much of the American public automatically sees bias in the press. Do we teach it in the schools? Because two centuries ago the American press by definition was partisan, does that legacy linger? It confounds and troubles me.

Len Downie, the executive editor of the *Washington Post*, goes to great lengths to keep any bias away from his news judgments. He won't even read his own paper's editorials so there is no chance they could influence his decisions on news coverage. He doesn't vote, for the same reason.

It doesn't matter; some still read bias into his coverage.

Max Frankel was once the editorial page editor of the *New York Times*—a famously liberal editorial page. His job was to write and supervise the writing of commentary that was almost always to the left of center. Then he was promoted to executive editor and his job was supervising news coverage that contained no bias.

I asked him once how he made the transition. I liked his answer.

"It's like going from being a lawyer—an advocate—to being a judge, where you cannot be an advocate," he said.

Exactly. But somehow vast numbers of readers don't grasp that. Somehow, because newspapers take editorial stands, readers think those views infiltrate news coverage. The guy who sat next to me at dinner knows I am the executive editor of this newspaper. I wondered if he thought I slant our front page toward my own biases. If he thinks the executive editor of the *New York Times* does, why wouldn't I?

It troubles me because there seems to be so much criticism directed at the media for assumed bias that I fear precious American rights could be in jeopardy. A University of Connecticut poll in May showed that seven in 10 Americans said it is important for the government to "hold the media in check."

And yet, the First Amendment was adopted by the Founding Fathers for just the opposite reason: so a free press and a free people can hold government in check. In other words, things are backwards.

If the people think the press is unfair or out of balance, then the next step is that their distrust could erode the historic role of the press as a watchdog on government. That would be a travesty.

What is bias? I maintain the front pages of the *New York Times* and *Washington Post* are not biased, but if readers believe they are—are they? How do you quantify it?

In the broadcast media, actually cablecast, Fox News Channel's main evening news show has come under criticism for a conservative bias. Fifty of 56 partisan guests interviewed on "Special Report with Brit Hume" over a five-month period earlier this year were Republicans, and only six were Democrats. Also, 65 of the show's 92 total guests were political conservatives, according to a study done by Fairness & Accuracy in Reporting, a liberal organization.

"Fox portrays itself as fair and balanced, as straight news," Steve Rendall, a FAIR senior analyst, told the AP. "It's media consumer fraud."

Hume said he would look into the group's findings, and correct it if he noticed any imbalance. FAIR monitored the news show during the first few months of a Republican administration, at a time the GOP also controlled Congress, and that played a part in the bookings, said Hume. "We don't strive for mathematical balance," he said. "We strive for an overall balanced outlook."

Executives at the cable network, which has been gaining on rival CNN in the ratings over the past few years, have always denied a right-wing tilt in news coverage.

FAIR also studied Wolf Blitzer's news program on CNN during the same period and found that of 67 partisan guests, 38 were Republicans and 29 were Democrats.

Though Hume's reaction is to defend his program's fairness, it would seem the numbers indicate a more balanced coverage by CNN.

When we talk of fairness, it means making sure that both—or all—sides of a story are presented. Sometimes one side can't be reached, so you point that out and follow it up the next day—or even hold the story to get the other side. Fairness needs to be measured not on just one day or one story, but on many days of coverage. If a news network is giving more air time to the leaders of one political party over another, it should change its ways.

But is there a deeper meaning to bias that readers are trying to get at? After all, human beings are by nature subjective. I maintain that most journalists—like judges, or scientists—try to put their subjective feelings aside in doing their jobs. Obviously a lot of people don't believe I can.

Can I? I bring everything that I am to my job—that, for example, I was raised in a small farming village populated only by white people. Someone who grew up in a city slum populated by only black people would bring a different set of life experiences to this job. Still another person, say a woman who spent most of her life in Puerto Rico, would bring something different. I don't think we can escape who we are, but what journalists must do is remember who they are and make sure they understand there are many more perspectives out there that have to get into the pages of the newspaper.

The editors who work with me know I'm a sucker for stories about outer space or prehistoric times. I call these "new knowledge" stories. A buried civilization found in ruins? Page One. A new galaxy discovered? Page One. Is that a bias? Another editor may relegate such stories to the back pages.

It is my call, but front-page decisions are made with several different editors in the room, all of us from different backgrounds with different personal beliefs. We keep each other journalistically honest.

The *Record-Journal* is a local newspaper and so most of our front page is filled most days with local stories—stories that *The Hartford Courant* or the *New Haven Register* would rarely, if ever, put on their front pages. We say that right up front—we're local. Is that a bias?

Yes it is, and I think it is an acceptable bias, like making a judgment that when mankind learns new things it is worth Page One.

What I don't do is let my personal political beliefs or the newspaper's editorial positions get in the way of news coverage. I find it frustrating that people don't believe that. Because this newspaper endorsed William Dickinson for mayor of Wallingford doesn't mean that I would plan only positive coverage of the mayor. The news needs to be impartial.

"Freedom of the press belongs to the people," states the American Society of Newspaper Editors Statement of Principles. "Good faith with the reader is the foundation of good journalism. Every effort must be made to assure that the news content is accurate, free from bias and in context, and that all sides are presented fairly," it continues.

I simply haven't met any editors who don't follow these precepts. Maybe they are out there, but they shouldn't be.

Here's a good development. The family of the founder of *The Boston Globe* has announced an award to recognize journalistic fairness. William O. Taylor, chairman emeritus of the *Globe*, and other members of his family raised $450,000 to endow the annual $10,000 Taylor Family Award for Fairness in Newspapers. It will be given out next year, based on work published in daily newspapers this year.

The Nieman Foundation for Journalism at Harvard University will administer the award.

There is no formal definition of fairness in the guidelines for the award nominations, which organizers say is deliberate. "The standards for fairness in journalism are complex and diverse and not easily defined for this kind of journalism competition," Bob Giles, curator of the Nieman Foundation, told the AP. "We anticipate there will be many ways to define work that can be held up as exemplary examples of fairness."

When even the profession has a hard time defining fairness, it is no wonder readers ask where it is.

But if there are questions about whether journalists value fairness, I'd hope that when one of the first families of American journalism endows a significant award in the name of fairness, it would go some way toward reassuring the public that fairness matters and bias is to be avoided.

If you see any coverage you think is biased, let me know. I'd be glad to discuss it with you.

July 8, 2001

When the kids teach the adults

WE ARE ALL sorting out our thoughts as we reel from the attacks of terrorists in New York and Washington. Just as it is the duty of firefighters, police and other emergency personnel to respond, it is the duty of the press to inform the public—to help us all understand our troubled world so we can come to knowledgeable decisions.

This newspaper, like every American newspaper, has put out pages and pages of coverage of the tragedy and of efforts locally to respond to the tragedy.

In one case, this newspaper had to report the news of two Meriden teachers suspended for "inappropriate comments" made to Palestinian-American students in their classrooms. This was a troubling development. We had published articles about the role of teachers in trying to explain the unimaginable to students, beginning with President Bush's hasty exit from an elementary school in Florida.

It is not an easy task for anyone, including teachers, and two here fumbled to the extent they were suspended without pay— one for one day, the other for three days.

So how does this newspaper get a full report to our readers on what happened in those classrooms? We are not strangers to covering schools and their students. Our reporters and photographers regularly talk to students and teachers on all kinds of subjects, from the routine to the difficult. Journalists are educated and trained to interview and discuss anything and everything with everyone. When it comes to students, especially minors, we have special guidelines.

"Give particular attention to preteens, especially in a news environment when they are out of their natural setting such as a classroom . . . report accurately and completely as possible . . . delicate situations require review by more than one editor. The burden is on us to make sure that we are not jeopardizing the child's safety or unnecessarily embarrassing him," states the *Record-Journal* policy on interviewing young students.

We have come under some criticism for interviewing students, including those who were in the classrooms and heard and saw what happened. That criticism includes charges of our "using" students or "leveraging" students, and even harming them because some of their friends avoid them now after they spoke the truth as they know it.

I would ask people to think about the six students we quoted.

I would ask them to consider that they were treated sensitively by trained journalists even when they were not treated sensitively by trained teachers. I would ask us to admire students who will defend fellow students when they are maligned by an authority figure. And I would ask us to value truth-tellers and truth-seekers and how important they are to a society dedicated to liberty.

It is the adults in this case who did not perform as well as the children. The adults—including the disciplined teachers, who were given every opportunity to explain their actions in our coverage and who chose to remain silent—refused to explain to the public what happened in their public schools.

Reread the sensitive, articulate and sensible remarks of the students we interviewed and be proud of them and defend them for their forthrightness.

"We don't hate Palestinians. . . . I thought it was kind of wrong. (The Palestinian-American student) was born in this country. . . . Teachers should be able to handle this without causing problems. . . . I think Ms. Chamberlain is still a great teacher, but she made a mistake. We all make mistakes. She shouldn't have been suspended."

Years from now, when these students are grown, they can look back on their published remarks and be confident that they were more thoughtful than the adults around them.

September 23, 2001

Remember what it stands for

WAVE THE FLAG but don't forget what it symbolizes from sea to shining sea. We've recited the pledge all our lives, but do we just mouth it or do we mean it: "with liberty and justice for all"? Is it rote or is it part of our hearts and minds?

When we wave the flag we wave, in a word, freedom. Do we know where freedom came from? Do we remember the effort against impossible odds it took to gain independence? And do we contemplate how hard it is to preserve life, liberty and pursuit of happiness?

From the shot heard 'round the world from Lexington and Concord in 1775, it was a long, precarious 15 years to declare our independence, defeat the most powerful nation on earth, establish a representative democracy and swear in the first Congress and president in 1790.

In those final two or three years when we wrote the U.S. Constitution that is the blueprint of our way of life, Thomas Jefferson from his ambassadorial post in Paris insisted that the right to freedom of speech and the press be included. He knew, as did the rest of the founders of this country, that a free people need to think and communicate freely. It is the essence of freedom—it is what the Stars and Stripes stand for. We wrote it down in our Bill of Rights, the first 10 amendments to the Constitution adopted in 1791.

Don't wave the flag if you don't know them. Look them up. They range from the right to own a gun to the right to a fair trial. The First Amendment alone has five freedoms. Do you know them?: freedom of speech, freedom of the press, freedom of religion, freedom of peaceable assembly and freedom to tell the government when it is doing something wrong, in the wording of the 18th century: "to petition the government for redress of grievances."

The American patriots had just told King George III to stick it. And we made it stick.

Certainly the sage of the revolution was Benjamin Franklin. He inspired all the rest when he wrote from the heart: "They that can give up essential liberty to obtain a little temporary safety deserve neither liberty nor safety."

The founding fathers of the United States of America knew they were not safe, that they were risking their lives to establish a nation based on principles that no other nation had ever been founded on. The British navy was in American waters, the British army was on American soil. The enemy's troops literally lived in the homes of the colonists. The danger to the rebels—that's what they were, rebels—was severe and real. A musket ball or a hangman's noose awaited all of them, unless they won.

When I heard Senate Majority Leader Tom Daschle say this week, after someone tried to kill him with anthrax, that democracy must go on, he made me think of Benjamin Franklin. Yes, Sen. Daschle was concerned about the members of his staff exposed to the deadly bacteria, and he urged precautions, but he was also angry and he was not backing down. The minority Republican leaders stood with him. We the people elected them and they were going to do their jobs as U.S. senators had for more than 200 years.

Sen. Daschle is a modern-day Franklin. He is a brave man and he reminds us that we must be brave. Tom Brokaw, Dan Rather and Peter Jennings, also targets of bio-terrorism, remind us that there is bravery among the leaders of the news media whose job it is to inform the people. If our duly elected leaders flinch, if the guardians of free speech and free press flinch, if the presses stop, the broadcasts end, if the Senate closes, the shot heard 'round the world may as well have been muzzled by a tyrannical monarch.

When you wave the flag, stand bravely and remember that if we erode the freedoms we stand for, then we stand for nothing; the flag is a mere piece of colored cloth blowing aimlessly in the wind.

October 21, 2001

— 2002 —

We'd better keep an eye on this

STEALING THE VIRGINITY of your leadoff hitter or your point guard when she is a teen-ager and you are her coach is reprehensible. So is dancing slow at a school dance and kissing a 14-year-old when you are her science teacher.

All the tawdry moves that many grown women are now saying their Southington teachers and coaches made on them in cars, in side rooms, in a motel room, in their homes—even on the playing field—are inexcusable. Adult predators going after the kids they are supposed to be teaching and mentoring would shock any community.

Just as disturbing is the evidence that nobody did anything about it. These women who finally came forward 15 and 20 years after they say it happened, also made it clear that it was an open secret, that those in charge had to know.

Did no one see basketball coach Joe Daddio walk into the girls' locker room? Did nobody question him doing that? Did no one see Joe Piazza during a tournament game put his hands in the "private area" of one of his players? Did they not know he was a "hands-on" coach? There are dozens of educators who were there then, still are and still partake in the see-no-evil, hear-no-evil mentality that these abused girls suffered through.

And what of the watchdog press? Three daily newspapers cover the town and its high school sports, but none of them broke any stories about coaches abusing their players. I was the sports editor of *The Hartford Courant* in the early 1980s. Southington was one of some 100 school districts we covered. I never heard a word of any improprieties there. The *R-J* then relied heavily on part-time freelancers, not the professionals of today.

Sportswriters love to cover games and shy away from controversies. If you go back far enough to the drinking and carousing of major league ballplayers when they rode trains between cities, you know that baseball writers never recorded any of it.

One night in Hartford at a Big East tournament we got word that Syracuse University basketball players had raped a Villanova cheerleader in their hotel room after a game. I told a staff writer to get over there and get the story. It wasn't about basketball; if he wanted to cover crime, he would have been a police reporter, was his attitude. I had to order him to get moving.

Sports departments are playfully referred to in the craft as the toy department. But even as we cover the unfolding story in Southington, it is our sports staff that is most appalled. All of us in the news business need to remind ourselves that if we truly care about the students we cover on a regular basis, our reportorial eyes and ears should have been more alert as we covered the storied teams and honored coaches of Southington. As Dan Rather has aptly put it, a reporter "is not an attack dog. Not a lapdog. But a watchdog."

There are honest and good men and women in the coaching ranks in Southington, just as there are honest and good journalists here. It is past time, however, for more vigilance.

Just as it is the business of a school principal or an athletic director to safeguard their students and players, it is the business of the press to be wise enough and alert enough to see when things aren't as they should be and to expose it.

We are mindful of the presumption of innocence and that the accused may never get their day in court. And we also ask whether anyone thinks these girls—now women—are making this up?

I am speaking for all of us here, sports writers and news reporters alike, that we are renewing our commitment to independent scrutiny and reassuring our readers that we are watching closely. If there are any coaches crazy enough to come on to any of their players in any inappropriate way, be forewarned.

January 13, 2002

Little white lies erode credibility

SOME READERS ARE after us for writing the truth. I am always dumbfounded when people can't bear the truth. A newspaper deserves criticism when it errs. When we get it right, I don't completely understand the condemnations.

The American public expects the truth from its newspapers, but last month several subscribers told us that we ought to be ashamed for writing in his obituary that former Wallingford Police Chief Carl A. Grasser pleaded guilty to obstruction of justice and resigned his position in 1969. He tried to cover up the arrest of a man accused of assaulting one of his own officers.

Mr. Grasser was a high public official in Wallingford and the career of a public official is just that—public. If he had retired with laurels instead of being forced to resign, we would have reported the laurels. But he didn't. Can you imagine leaving out of Richard Nixon's obituary that he resigned from the presidency? Can you imagine when Sen. Ted Kennedy dies, ignoring the bridge at Chappaquiddick?

Those who called or wrote asked why we couldn't concentrate on the good in Chief Grasser's life. We did. We wrote that he was "an innovative chief," a "devoted family man," a "devoted husband," an "active parishioner" in his church. We quoted a former town attorney who said he was "a good police officer," "very kind," and "led a very exemplary life" after he left the department. We quoted former Mayor William Bertini that he regretted having had to take action against the police chief.

This is one disconnect between the press and the public that is difficult to resolve. There seems to be a feeling that we should not speak ill of the dead. Certainly, not every misdeed in a person's life has to be recorded in the last story written about him or her. Minor blemishes are not newsworthy. If a police chief, for example, had been suspended for a day only once back when he was a sergeant over a small departmental violation, it probably shouldn't be included in a story about his whole life.

The *New York Times Manual of Style and Usage*, a highly regarded reference work in the industry, gives this guidance for obituaries: "If a crime or indiscretion was the subject's main claim to fame, it should of course figure in the lead (first paragraph). But an early indiscretion should be kept in proportion— subordinated or omitted, depending on its ultimate significance in a life."

I sympathize with family and friends who do not want to read about Chief Grasser's resignation, but it was a wholly significant event in his life and my responsibility is to the tens of thousands of readers of this newspaper who expect the *Record-Journal* to present truthful accounts. If we receive 10 complaints, it means some 65,000 other readers did not complain, so perhaps this is a sermon to the choir.

Someone's life is not black and white. To trot out only platitudes, to pretend that unpleasant things never happen in a life, to deny the complexity of life is almost an insult to a human being.

I should mention that this newspaper has a paid obituary policy whereby a family submits an obituary through a funeral home that includes information they choose and leaves out information they do not want. These notices appear on the obituary page for a fee, which allow a family to virtually dictate what will and will not be in the obit.

The *Record-Journal* also assigns news obituaries on prominent people. It is in these news articles that we are duty-bound to follow the dictates and judgments of sound journalism. We simply would not be upholding our responsibility to our readers if we started withholding significant information about prominent public officials. That kind of editing leads to erosion of trust with our readers.

March 10, 2002

Everything offends somebody

HERE'S AN IDEA. Let's take all the accountants and have them do the judging and take all the judges to do all the accounting. The accountants will decide what justice is and the judges will decide what is good financial practice.

We could take all the political operatives and have them do the journalism and have journalists do all the politicking. The politicians will decide what news is and the journalists will run our governments.

Farmers could do the engineering and engineers do all the farming. Teachers could do the policing and cops do the teaching. Diplomats could do all the fighting and soldiers do all the diplomacy. Probably wouldn't work, though. For sure, editors could not run our town, state or federal governments.

You may have noticed that a political operative, and others, wrote to us last week that a state senator's divorce is not news and how dare we print it. It is hard enough finding good people to fill the ranks of politics and government without them having to worry if their divorce shows up in the paper, says he. David Fordiani is a skillful political operative and was a key player in the Democrats' loss of the Meriden mayorship. But I would suggest he stick to politics and we'll stick to what is news.

Since 1776, in this country it has been a given that if you become a public official or public figure, what you do and say will become news. That is our system. That is our democracy. Anyone who wants to get involved should understand that. America stands for journalists deciding what is published—not anybody else deciding, certainly not the government.

Inside a newspaper, we have deep and long discussions about what to print and what not to print. Often that gets into how much of a public person's private life should the voting public know about. We have been told that a president having sex in the Oval Office is nobody's business. We disagree. We have been told that a governor's divorce is nobody's business. We disagree. And we disagree that a state senator's divorce is not news. It is.

Sen. Thomas Gaffey, D-Meriden, has said his divorce has held up thousands of dollars in reimbursements for his personal expenses to his employer, the scandal-wracked CRRA. Sen. Gaffey himself did not object to the *Record-Journal* reporting his divorce.

Because a state senator makes the laws under which we all live, because a state senator has power over you and me, because a state senator, like a governor or a president or a city councilor decides policy—his or her character, his or her thinking, his or her makeup is important for the public to know.

Marital status is part of a person's makeup. Divorce is not good or bad; it can be both. I was divorced. I have written that my four daughters are part of a melded family. I do not make public policy, but I make decisions on how much you will know about the policymakers. If the policymakers don't like that, they are living in the wrong country.

If you don't like a certain story, turn the page. I guarantee you will find something you like. It is sort of like listening to the radio. If a song comes on you don't like, change the station. Every day a newspaper prints things that are upsetting to someone. And every day a newspaper prints things that are satisfying, even uplifting to someone.

Life on this planet is troubling, exciting, uplifting, sad, happy, horrifying, beautiful. If a newspaper is supposed to reflect life and if you are reading a newspaper that does not portray horror, beauty, happiness, sadness, excitement or trouble—if it doesn't uplift you and make you laugh or make you cry—what kind of newspaper is that? It is an irrelevancy at your doorstep every morning. It is not worth your time. It is bland and blank and missing the parade of life as it goes by.

May 5, 2002

Don't tread on my freedom

LAST SUNDAY WE published nearly 5,000 words on a dispute this newspaper is having with the Meriden Police Department. We retained a respected freelance writer to research and write the piece and arranged for Associated Press editors in Hartford to edit the story. We could have written and edited it ourselves, but chose to engage outside journalists to scrutinize the issue in order to present the most objective account we could.

Freelancer Alan Bisbort of Cheshire, who has written for *The Washington Post* and *The New York Times* and has authored 14 books, interviewed city police officers, *Record-Journal* personnel, and independent experts. The different points of view—that police think they may arrest reporters for harassment; that journalists think covering news cannot lead to harassment charges—were presented fully.

I believe that most of our readers see the value of telling them the story of this dispute and understand the importance of a free press. It troubles me when some readers write letters about how we are "hiding behind the First Amendment" or that we are "veiled in the cloak of First Amendment rights." Such language cheapens the Bill of Rights. It makes me wonder if some Americans don't understand how crucial those rights are to our way of life.

We all need to consider how dangerous it is to let armed police handcuff journalists for asking questions in the pursuit of news. Writing news is no easy task. Minions stand in the way, do everything they can to prevent the truth from coming out. Reporters must ask questions, they must ask tough questions and they often have to ask the questions repeatedly in order to do what our society has appointed the news media to do: inform. You cannot have a democracy without a free press. You cannot have a free press if the police can round up reporters for doing their job.

We hear much lately about the right to privacy. There is no right to privacy listed in the Bill of Rights. You will not find the word privacy anywhere in the U.S. Constitution. The Founding Fathers enumerated the people's rights in the first 10 amendments—from freedom of speech to the right to a fair trial—but were silent about privacy.

The modern legal theory of privacy began with an 1890 *Harvard Law Review* essay co-authored by Louis Brandeis, who later became a Supreme Court justice. He argued that people have the "right to be left alone," but also held "the right to privacy does not prohibit any publication of matter which is of public or general interest."

We should welcome the balancing act of conflicting liberties, but we should not let the police make those decisions. It is in the civil courts, not criminal courts, where Constitutional disputes are settled.

We were mindful of the privacy of Fire Chief William Dunn's wife and family after the tragedy of his suicide, offering the opportunity to comment if they chose. But some criticize us even for asking the chief, after he took a leave, why he did. The fire chief is charged with protecting city residents from danger. He manages a $6 million budget and a staff of 114. Of course the public should know why he needed a leave, and the way the public finds out is by the newspaper asking why.

In a 1988 Washington State case where an official sued a reporter (he did not try to have the reporter arrested) on harassment grounds, the judge ruled in favor of the reporter because to find otherwise "would constitute an unwarranted interference in the newsgathering process in violation of the First Amendment."

In Meriden last month, the fact that the state's attorney tossed the warrant out should be proof enough that the police were off base in seeking to arrest our reporter.

September 8, 2002

Do the police have a right to censor the news?

MERIDEN DEPUTY POLICE Chief Jeffry Cossette asked me for a retraction on the last paragraph of my column last Sunday.

I wrote: "In Meriden last month, the fact that the state's attorney tossed the warrant out should be proof enough that the police were off base in seeking to arrest our reporter."

The arrest warrant wasn't submitted to the state's attorney, the deputy chief wrote to me in an e-mail.

I'm not sure how crucial it is whether the warrant formally went to the prosecutor or not. Clearly the cops went to the prosecutor.

The deputy chief was quite incensed, however. He called it a "fabricated statement," a "cheap shot" with "no factual basis" and said I was unethical and unprofessional for writing it.

I should have been more precise in that last sentence. Instead of writing that it was a fact that the state's attorney threw the warrant out, I should have pointed out what was reported in this paper the week before: "The legal matter is unresolved. It appears the state's attorney's office has rejected a police application for the arrest of (a reporter), but officials refuse to confirm or deny that."

Deputy Chief Cossette is now denying it. "The arrest warrant was never submitted to the state's attorney. Therefore, it was never 'thrown out,'" he wrote.

Freelance writer Alan Bisbort, in his Sept. 1 story, quoted the deputy chief saying that the police "had sent the matter on to the state's attorney." Mr. Cossette says now that he wasn't referring to the warrant affidavit.

I asked Mr. Bisbort if the deputy chief or the chief, William Abbatematteo, said anything else on the subject. The writer checked his notes. In the hour-long, wide-ranging interview with the two top Meriden cops, one or the other also said: "Legally, it's in the hands of the state's attorney's office, whose job it is to enforce criminal law." Also: "Whether it's a criminal matter is not up to us. We send it on to the state's attorney. . . ." Also: "Normally we send these matters on to the state's attorney." Also: "The state's attorney suggested that we get the family's attorney to send a letter to the newspaper."

That last point interested me, because it is exactly what I suggested to Deputy Chief Cossette, that if someone is upset with the newspaper, he can always take civil action, which is not a matter for the police. It then goes directly to a judge.

Once more, for the record, here is the crux of the controversy: The police tried to arrest one of our reporters because he contacted Meriden firefighter Ryan Dunn. The reporter called him to offer him the chance to comment on the official police report on the suicide of Fire Chief William Dunn, Ryan's father. The newspaper maintains that out of fairness and sensitivity, reporters must do everything they can to give those involved in news stories the opportunity to comment. The police have called it alleged harassment and say that if they receive a complaint, they can arrest reporters for doing it.

Chief Dunn's widow had told us she preferred not to comment, so we never contacted her. His son Ryan said at various times that he wanted to, and that he didn't want to, comment.

Assistant State's Attorney James Dinnan told Mr. Bisbort that if his office rejects an arrest warrant application, he will not comment. He refused comment except to say there is no legal case pending against a *Record-Journal* reporter.

The stance Abbatematteo and Cossette are taking should be troubling to everyone. If you follow their logic, anytime someone is upset at being asked questions by a reporter, they can call the cops and get the reporter arrested.

So let's say Monica Lewinsky didn't want reporters asking her questions. Just call the cops and charge harassment. Stop the story in its tracks.

But this case is about a human tragedy. Both police officers and reporters serve essential functions in society, especially in times of tragedy. Police and reporters often work together in tragic situations. Tragedies like the deaths of thousands in two towers in New York. Tragedies like the death of one fire chief in Meriden. In order to do their work, police must ask a lot of questions in the midst of tragedy. In order to do our work, reporters must ask a lot of questions in the midst of tragedy.

So consider the Abbatematteo/Cossette stance that if someone is upset in a tragedy over being interviewed by a journalist,
all they need do is complain to the cops, who then can go after
warrants for the arrest of the journalist. How, then, could reporters write about what happened at the World Trade Center?
How can reporters help a community, a nation, comprehend,
understand, fathom what is going on, if cops can carry them off
and prevent them from telling the stories?

It is difficult to interview grieving people. It is sometimes
difficult for grieving people to express their thoughts and feelings. But journalists give them the opportunity to do that. Quite
often, grief-stricken people want to; they find it cathartic, they
want to say something important about the loved one who is
gone. They honor the deceased by sharing with others what was
good and meaningful about them. Read the poignant "Portraits
of Grief" in the *New York Times* about the victims at the World
Trade Center and you will know the power of good reporting.
Or read the compassionate coverage in words and pictures in
this newspaper of a courageous fireman, William Dunn.

Our reporters do not harass people who are grieving; they
give them a chance to express themselves. In doing that, they
allow the public to read a more human story and a more com-
prehensible story.

In his e-mail to me, the deputy chief wrote, "The complainant did not want to pursue charges at this time . . . If you had
obtained a copy of the police report, this factual information
would have been available to you." And "If you had done the
proper research and obtained your information as to how the
case was closed, you would have learned the truthful conclusion
to the case."

I was gratified that the complainant withdrew his complaint,
which Mr. Bisbort reported on Sept. 1. The police provided
us their report Friday. It left out an important fact about the
"truthful conclusion to the case." It didn't mention that City
Manager Roger Kemp told the chief and deputy chief to stop

any and all action against *Record-Journal* reporters until the city attorney (who is different from the state's attorney) looks into it. In other words, until City Attorney Larry Kendzior examines the constitutional—civil, not criminal—case law, the police are to stand down.

Mr. Kemp hired Chief Abbatematteo. The city manager is the police chief's boss and he told him to cease and desist. It is always a good idea in a democracy to have civilians in charge of police.

Deputy Chief Cossette told me that his department is "a professional organization committed to public service." So is this organization.

Anyone who breaks the law, including journalists, should be arrested. But no one here is breaking any laws, and the police should have known that from the very beginning. This newspaper and the police department have served this community together for more than a century, and the relationship has historically been a good one.

Recently, Deputy Chief Cossette organized a media relations seminar for his command staff. Some of our staff participated. That's a good step. I have told him and the chief that we are willing to meet at any time to discuss differences.

Given Mr. Kemp's directive, I am hopeful this dispute is behind us.

September 15, 2002

Teaching the wrong lessons

MAYBE YOU READ the other day that Southington School Superintendent Harvey Polansky kicked a reporter out of his office. Harvey is a big bear of a guy who has told us he runs an open administration. Caroline Porter is a smidgen, but she carries big questions. Too big for the superintendent, apparently.

Meanwhile in Wallingford, a usually reasonable public personage asked a reporter not to talk to any members of the town's Wooding-Caplan study committee. He should limit himself to writing only what is discussed at formal committee meetings, this committee member said. The Town Council appointed the committee to figure out what to do with the uptown property, which has sat dormant since the town bought it in 1991 for $1.5 million.

This disregard by public officials for informing the public is frightening.

Educators especially have a heavy responsibility to teach the American way of life—the importance of a free and unfettered press to Americans. It is a basic freedom, isn't it, that we all stand for and fight for and die for, in how many wars, when our way of life is threatened?

Isn't it the First Amendment—the first!—in our Bill of Rights?

What does it say to our students when our leading educators decide that what happens in the public schools is private—none of the public's business? Dr. Polansky not only kicked a reporter out; he chastised her for interviewing teachers and students about issues in the schools.

Now tell me, who else should reporters talk to about what is happening inside the schools other than teachers and students—and, of course, administrators, if they choose to answer questions? The saddest thing in Southington is that it was merely about why the police officer assigned to the high school was suddenly reassigned. Will somebody tell me why that is such a sensitive topic?

Maybe we all just want the official versions, the spin, the half-truths of officialdom—no need for independent scrutiny by an inquiring press. Never mind that a vigorous and inquiring press is one of the foundations of our free society.

"Freedom of the press belongs to the people. It must be defended against encroachment or assault from any quarter, public or private," states the American Society of Newspaper Editor's "Statement of Principles," which has stood since the 1920s, when it was adopted.

"The American press was made free not just to inform or just to serve as a forum for debate, but also to bring an independent scrutiny to bear on the forces of power in the society, including the conduct of official power at all levels of government."

If this isn't being taught in Dr. Polansky's schools, it sure ought to be.

Translate the Wallingford official's idea on how to cover the local committee to Henry Kissinger's committee looking into the failures of our national security apparatus. What if the rules were that reporters could not ask Dr. Kissinger any questions, that reporters could not talk to committee members, all they could do was listen at their official meetings?

What kind of media would sit back and publish only the official version? The Iraqi press, for one. The German press in the 1930s and 1940s for another.

The ASNE code also dictates that "journalists must be constantly alert to see that the public's business is conducted in public." We take these principles seriously because so many people who rise to high public office forget so easily that the American system is all about freedom, including the independent scrutiny provided by a free press.

December 15, 2002

— 2003 —

We are committed to diversity

AH, THE MAIL. I love mailboxes, I love e-mail. In newspapers, I love the letters to the editor—they are a community talking to itself, the wonderful resonance of a democratic people.

And when someone writes accusing me, 1) of the sin of silence, 2) of agreeing with my colleague Glenn Richter over there on the right, and 3) accusing this newspaper of employing too few minority journalists, I like to write back.

Amateur local historian (and a good one) Colleen Cyr wrote that triple whammy in one letter published Friday.

Mr. Richter and I agree on precious little, politically speaking, but we do agree that "Trying to make the workplace look more like America is a good idea," as he wrote last week. His emphasis has been to advocate American grit and self-reliance, while I always add the necessary ingredient of racial justice and tolerance, which, sadly, this country hasn't always provided.

Mr. Richter was writing of flaws in *New York Times* management, which was not diligent enough in editing a black reporter who made up stories. The reporter was fired and, five weeks later, the top two *Times* editors resigned for mishandling that one errant employee and for larger failings that affected morale at the famed newspaper.

Ms. Cyr saw in Mr. Richter's column a lack of commitment here to minority hiring.

We can always do better, but our goal was and is to make sure our News department's staff reflects the diversity of our market. We do that through recruiting, training and a highly successful minority internship/scholarship program.

I took great pride last week in the well-deserved promotion of Ratnanjali Beniwal to features editor. She is of Asian Indian descent, our very first recipient of the internship/scholarship after she graduated from Meriden's Maloney High School and went on to study journalism at Southern Connecticut State University. She would be the first to insist that her work be judged on its merits, not on her heritage.

Yet we recognize that a newspaper, perhaps more than other organizations because it has the responsibility to look at the world from all possible angles, benefits from editors, reporters and photographers who are not all one vanilla flavor. Different points of view, different backgrounds, different upbringings, different cultures enrich a newsroom as much as they enrich a school, a community, a nation.

This summer, among a half-dozen college interns, two young women of color are following in Ms. Beniwal's footsteps.

My "silence" last Sunday over what Mr. Richter had to say was because I thought I had something important to say about another issue: war and peace. But any casual reader of this column will know that over the years I have been anything but silent about racial justice and equality in the land of the free.

Mr. Richter wrote that *Times* Executive Editor Howell Raines "damaged any number of minority journalists yet to come . . . by applying different standards of behavior to different people, according to race."

To me, that is the key. Once hired, each employee must be given every opportunity to succeed, but in the end, it is the employee himself or herself who accomplishes that feat through diligent and good work under standards of performance set equally for all.

It was a sad day for journalism when Mr. Raines resigned only a year after his staff won a record seven Pulitzer prizes. But, as the *Wall Street Journal* put it, "he consolidated power and control within a coterie of confidants and pet reporters, intensifying a culture that discouraged dissent."

Fatal in a newsroom.

June 8, 2003

Competing views on bias in the press

NEWSPAPERS ARE MORE conservative than liberal.

The present blip in the media bias debate—it never really ends, because there are as many views on bias as there are viewers and readers—is taking place in one of those cyclical societal swings to the right. Americans, since we became Americans, have swung back and forth over our history, leaning left, then leaning right, then swinging back to the center.

The press, just a part of the "media" now, has been a fulcrum for this tugging and pulling—sometimes leading the way, sometimes following, sometimes merely observing.

Conservatives have always loved to complain that the press is too liberal, and liberals have held that the press is too conservative. To me, that is too simple.

The press was biased and partisan for most of our history and served the nation well. Less than a hundred years ago, in the early 20th century, the press itself—newspaper editors and publishers—decided to become more "objective" and less partisan. Editors adopted ethics codes calling for fairness and balance in coverage. It's important to remember that the press itself did this. Nobody made editors do it. Dating back at least to the adoption of the Bill of Rights in 1791, government does not tell the press what to do. Newspapers and news media are there to watch the government—not the other way around.

Today, our great bias debate between conservatives and liberals is too confining. Aren't there biases that are acceptable? A majority of Americans would agree that democracy is better than monarchy, for example. But that is, without a doubt, a bias.

Ever since the Chicago humorist and columnist Finley Peter Dunne wrote in 1902 that the newspaper "comforts the afflicted, afflicts the comfortable," Americans have identified with his idea, which is another bias. Turn it around—should newspapers comfort the comfortable and afflict the afflicted?

I would submit the press has done both since Dunne's day. The muckraking press then exposed appalling poverty in city slums, degraded conditions in "insane asylums," and public health threats in meat-packing industries, to name a few.

But the press also has ignored afflictions such as racial segregation in everything from major league baseball to voting booths in the South. The news media did next to nothing to expose the great injustices of segregation until people like Rosa Parks and Martin Luther King Jr. began a movement. Then, I would argue, TV and newspapers were instrumental in changing society for the better by covering the civil rights movement and advocating for change.

But even then, the mainstream press was cautious. The *New York Times* refused to publish Martin Luther King's "Letter from Birmingham Jail," one of the most significant documents in American history and certainly among the most provocative. The *Times* comforted the comfortable by urging black leaders to go slow, while King's 1963 letter demanded immediate action.

In the present liberal/conservative feud over bias in the press, I believe newspapers are more conservative than liberal, more a part of the power structure than an instrument of change. The vast majority of newspaper publishers are more conservative than liberal and, over the years, more of them endorsed Republican presidential candidates than Democrats.

Conservatives, by definition, favor the status quo and are quick to criticize a press they see as "activist." To me, making news judgments to write about injustice is one of the highest purposes of a free press. As a kid, watching Superman (a.k.a. Clark Kent) on TV gave me goose bumps when the music was underscored by the rousing words that the man of steel was out to defend "truth, justice and the American way."

If you believe that segregation was wrong, then you must believe that justice was not always the American way. We ought to acknowledge, too, that America does not have a monopoly on truth and justice. We are better today than many nations, but we are not the only democracy on earth. Concepts like justice and liberty transcend nationhood.

The Pew Research Center for the People and the Press delved into the nature of global news gathering and how people perceive it in a study released last month. It reported that seven in 10 Americans see it as a good thing when news organizations take a "strong pro-American point of view." However, when asked if it is better for coverage of the war on terrorism to be neutral or pro-American, 64 percent favor neutral coverage.

This is a large question with roots in a belief that truth trumps patriotism. And what is pro-American, anyway? Is Bill Clinton's view of global warming or George Bush's view of global warming, the American point of view? Is President Nixon's invasion of Cambodia or Sen. George McGovern's criticism of the invasion, the American way? Or, more recently, is President Bush's invasion of Iraq, or citizens and senators who protested the invasion, more American?

Your choice, but at least see that the pursuit of the truth helps you make your choice. Whether you think the present administration is blind to greenhouse gases or not, shouldn't you support a free press that will look into the issue and inform the public about the scientific research as well as the political debate?

Much is made of the group-think in the nation's news-rooms—the idea that the news media is a monolith filled with the followers of FDR or JFK. I can tell you this newsroom is anything but. We have regular churchgoers and atheists, Asians, Anglos, Latinos, Jews, Catholics, Protestants, libertarians, so-cialists, conservatives, liberals, suburbanites, urbanites, grandfa-thers and grandmothers, editors and reporters raising children, and single young men and women just out of college, and on and on.

With a melting pot like that—and it is the same at virtually all daily newspapers—it is hard to push any one agenda. In all that diversity in newsrooms large and small, we put our per-sonal beliefs aside to make news judgments, much as jurors do in following the law and evidence to reach a decision.

Bias is simply the wrong word. Journalists are one-minded in pursuing stories to get at the truth, wherever it leads. It is an elusive target but a noble pursuit. Storytelling is its own excuse for being. Writing distinguishes us as human. It is an eloquent mark of civilization. Writing the news and expressing opinions about the news and newsmakers is journalism's great contribu-tion every day to life on earth.

August 3, 2003

§ No secret trials here, thank you

WHEN A STATE prosecutor called this newspaper irresponsible for naming and describing prospective jurors in a criminal case, I respectfully disagreed. Jurors in the American criminal justice system have been part of the public process of justice ever since the system was established.

Senior Assistant State's Attorney James R. Dinnan in Meriden Superior Court filed a brief last week accusing the *Record-Journal* of acting "in an irresponsible fashion by publishing the personal information of jurors" and destroying "any semblance of privacy that remains."

In his brief, Mr. Dinnan told Superior Court Judge Stephen Frazzini that, according to the Connecticut (Judicial) Practice Book, juror questionnaires "will be held confidential" and information provided by jurors "is for the sole purpose" of determining whether they would be "appropriate" to sit in judgment. He further stated it is not the "intent that their name, identifying characteristics or personal information be publicly disclosed."

If he really thinks all that, what court system has he been practicing in? Jurors deliberate in private but are chosen in public. The questionnaires may be confidential, but any officer of the court knows they are designed for lawyers to ask all sorts of questions in open court. Lawyers know that anything said in open court is public, and purposely so.

The prosecutor, representing the people (who pay his salary) will try to persuade jurors that the alleged criminal Judith Scruggs is responsible for her son hanging himself and that she ought to be thrown in jail for up to 10 years.

The defense lawyer, M. H. Reese Norris of Hartford, will try to persuade the jury that Mrs. Scruggs is innocent and that her boy, J. Daniel Scruggs, suffered merciless bullying at school.

Anyone who thinks those who make decisions should be anonymous in the serious business of a criminal trial just doesn't grasp the basic principles of justice in a free society. Are there rare exceptions—a witness in Mafia trials who could be endangered, for example? Yes. There are no such exceptions here.

If you are a juror performing your duty as a citizen, you shouldn't want to be anonymous, and judges and lawyers shouldn't want them to be.

The Sixth Amendment, the "fair trial" amendment in the Bill of Rights adopted in 1791, guarantees the right to a "speedy and public trial." A defendant, whose lawyer helps select the jurors, has every right to know who the people are who will decide guilt or innocence.

Those in government, whether it is executive, legislative or judicial, often would prefer secrecy. But in our system—especially criminal justice, where we decide the fate of individual citizens—secrecy is a miscarriage of justice.

Opposing counsel in this case are asking prospective jurors if they have ever dealt with suicide, mental problems, bullying, or even messy bedrooms. These are questions they should be asking so they and the judge can decide if a person is fit to serve on this case.

The people, through the press whose job it is to cover the courts—indeed to be a watchdog over the courts—have every right to know who is deciding if Judith Scruggs is criminally responsible for her son's death.

Judge Frazzini has already told Mr. Dinnan that his first brief was too broad and to go back and rethink it. The judge will hear arguments in open court Tuesday morning. I'm sure he is mindful of the tug and pull between our First Amendment right to a free press and our Sixth Amendment right to a fair trial. They have been in conflict before, and our system has performed well with that balance.

To me, anonymous jurors in this case would be an abuse of the system.

September 14, 2003

No secrecy needed in free society

I WALKED INTO the Meriden Public Library to look up my favorite trial—John Peter Zenger's in New York City. There in the Children's Department was *The Trial of John Peter Zenger, August 1735, An Early Fight for America's Freedom of the Press*, by Frank B. Latham.

On Page 46 is this: "The jury was quickly selected, and their names caused a stir of excitement in the courtroom. They were: Thomas Hunt, foreman; Samuel Weaver, Stanley Holmes, John Bell, Egbert van Borsom, John Goelet, Harmanus Rutgers, Benjamin Hildreth, Edward Man, Andreis Marschalk, Abraham Ketelas, and Hercules Wendover."

No one was worried that the jurors were publicly chosen and named. To the contrary, there was excitement because a majority was of Dutch ancestry and might actually find in favor of the German immigrant printer Zenger.

How satisfying it is to find in our libraries books instructive in the fundamentals of American liberties so readily available to children of the 21st century.

Two things: 1) the jury found Zenger, who published the *New York Weekly Journal*, innocent of seditious libel against the government, and established for the first time that printing the truth was a defense against charges of libel; 2) it all happened before there was a United States and reminds us that our liberties run deep in the roots of the country.

You may notice all the jurors were men, and white men. It wasn't until well into the 20th century that women and black people were allowed to serve on juries. Today every woman and every black person selected to serve should relish the chance, remember that their grandmothers never got the chance, and proudly shout it from the rooftops—I am doing my public duty as a citizen! A public not a private duty.

It is astonishing that our own Internet poll (unscientific as it is) shows that citizens today by a 10-to-1 margin think jurors' names should be kept secret. Not enough people are going to the library to brush up on our basic rights: First Amendment—free speech and press; Sixth Amendment—public trial; Seventh Amendment—the right to trial by jury.

Do not take these lightly. They and the other rights guaranteed in our Bill of Rights of 1791 are what we stand for as a people. Be wary of those who want to make things secret in a free society.

Trial by jury developed out of a fear that trial by government—king, sheik, emperor, dictator, even judge—had too much room for abuse, star chamber justice. When your peers decide your guilt or innocence, we believe you have a better chance at a fair trial. And so we offer on this page Superior Court Judge Stephen Frazzini's decision last week that the names of the jurors in the *State v. Judith Scruggs* will be made public.

As a reporter and editor for 34 years, with rare exceptions I have made sure that jurors remain public and true to the Sixth Amendment guarantee of a "public trial." As a juror myself once in a criminal trial, I tried to make sure the men and women serving with me performed our duty well.

A loud yahoo got himself appointed foreman and declared no need for discussion. The culprit was clearly guilty, he said, and called for a vote. The judge had reminded the jury of the need for deliberation. We voted anyway without discussion. So I did the only thing I could do. I voted not guilty. It was 5 to 1. We stayed and deliberated and deliberated.

The defendant faced two counts. Through discussion I was persuaded there was no reasonable doubt that he was guilty of the first count. Second count, it was 5 to 1 again. Through deliberation, the other five eventually joined me. We declared him innocent of the second count. That's the American system.

September 21, 2003

§ Two rights don't make a wrong

THE GREAT WISDOM of the Founding Fathers is unfolding before our very eyes in Meriden Superior Court. The historic tug and pull, the clash of competing American rights, featured Friday five lawyers, three reporters, one juror, one defendant, and the judge working his way to a decision on whether that defendant, Judith Scruggs, received a fair trial.

That decision hinges in part, the defense argues, on what one of the jurors said to the press.

As lawyers for *The Hartford Courant*, *The New York Times* and the *Record-Journal* appeared in court Friday, arguing to protect reporters from being forced to testify, Superior Court Judge Stephen F. Frazzini said from the bench that whether questioning reporters is "properly permitted" involves "weighty issues that I am not going to decide today."

It is free press v. fair trial, the First Amendment of the Bill of Rights v. the Sixth Amendment, and there is long precedent and case law to guide the fray. Judge Frazzini asked for more briefs and set a hearing for Dec. 19.

Daniel J. Klau of Hartford, the *Record-Journal*'s attorney in this case, referred to several federal and state cases dating back to 1972 that show reporters can be compelled to testify only if the information sought is not "reasonably attainable from other available sources."

The lawyer for Mrs. Scruggs, who was convicted of risk of injury after her 12-year-old son Daniel committed suicide, is seeking testimony from the reporters after two of them, including Rachel Makwana of the *Record-Journal*, wrote stories that juror Vincent Giardina said he considered information not put into evidence in coming to a guilty verdict. The defense calls that grounds for mistrial.

Mr. Klau argued in his brief that on a practical level "the question the court needs to answer is 'What went on in Mr. Giardina's head?' Only Mr. Giardina knows the answer to that question. Asking Ms. Makwana and her fellow reporters to confirm what they wrote will do nothing more than establish that Mr. Giardina made conflicting statements."

The *Times* reported on Oct. 12 that "Mr. Giardina said he supported a conviction, in part, because he did not want Ms. Scruggs to sue the city if she were acquitted." Ms. Makwana of the *Record-Journal* asked Giardina if the *Times'* report was true. He was quoted as saying in her Oct. 14 article, "I would by lying if I said it wasn't," and added that he would hate to see Mrs. Scruggs profit from her son's death. The *Courant* reported on Oct. 29 that Giardina said a Scruggs suit "definitely was not on my mind during deliberations."

"In criminal cases, post-verdict questioning of jurors by the media about their deliberations is common," argued Mr. Klau. "The public has a right to know why jurors rendered the verdict that they did. Such knowledge bears on the integrity of the criminal justice system. However, if such reporting puts journalists at constant risk of being subpoenaed in connection with a post-verdict motion for acquittal or new trial, the chilling effect on the media cannot be discounted."

In other words, if in doing their job journalists can be hauled into court any time someone questions their work, it weakens the First Amendment, which guarantees us a "vigorous, aggressive and independent press" in the words of the New York federal appeals court that rejected attempts to put reporters on the witness stand in 1972.

Upholding a fair trial here is about finding the answer to what a juror was thinking when he voted to convict. Questioning reporters won't provide that answer. One right is not more important than the other. Fair trial and free press are equally important to our democracy. There is no need to chip away at the First Amendment here to attain a fair trial.

November 16, 2003

§ There's room for this one

"THE BOONDOCKS," THE comic strip featuring black kids, took a beating in our informal and admittedly unscientific poll. More than 300 readers, a large number for such efforts, let us know their favorites and unfavorites in the funnies. Overwhelmingly, Aaron McGruder's "The Boondocks" was an unfavorite.

Readers thought it was angry, hard to understand, not funny, though some acknowledged it was satirical, and belonged—if we must publish it—on the editorial pages. A few readers praised it, and us for running it.

I love my First Amendment calendar. Each day there's a nugget worth reading. Nov. 5 was this from a college student: "If you are not prepared to read ideas that are not your own and that you might disagree with, you do not belong at an institution of higher learning."

I'd add, never mind reading a newspaper. That may sound blunt, but please consider the value of reading ideas not your own, reading opinions you disagree with—that is how we grow as individuals. That is how I feel about "The Boondocks."

As a kid, Aaron McGruder would draw over and over in "endless attempts to capture Snoopy with my own hand." Peanuts creator Charles M. Schulz "taught me how to be a human being," Mr. McGruder has said. Bloom County creator Berkeley Breathed "taught me how to be a cartoonist," Calvin and Hobbes creator Bill Watterson "taught me how to tell a joke, Schulz taught me which jokes to tell.

"These were my first life lessons. Be down with the underdog, empathize with the victimized, life isn't always fair, Christmas is too commercial . . . girls will pull away at the last second and leave you screaming flat on your back," he said.

He also remembered Mr. Schulz saying the odds of getting syndicated as a cartoonist was several thousand to one and "I quickly wrote that off as a possible career choice." But at the University of Maryland he put out his first "Boondocks" in the student paper. He earned his degree in Afro-American studies and at age 25, in 1999, succeeded at national syndication.

Film maker (*Bowling for Columbine*) and author (*Stupid White Men*) Michael Moore wrote the forward to Mr. McGruder's book *A Right to be Hostile, The Boondocks Treasury*: "With bodacious wit, in just a few panels, each day Aaron serves up . . . life in America through the eyes of two African-American kids who are full of attitude, intelligence, and rebellion. Each time I read the strip, I laugh—and I wonder . . . how on earth can the most truthful thing in the newspaper be the comics?"

In an interview with the *Philadelphia City Paper* two years ago, Mr. McGruder said, "I think the strip challenges people to think differently, and that to me is far more important than to have people thinking like me—I want to have people questioning what they're told on a daily basis."

"The whole reason I created the strip in the first place," he said, was "because I wanted to see some black people in a decent comic strip."

How come Huey and Riley always look so angry? is a frequently asked question on his Web site.

Mr. McGruder responds: "It will be clearer as the strip develops, but Huey never smiles. He's too busy contemplating the hypocrisies of the world. Riley rarely smiles, but he might crack a smirk if doing something particularly tyrannical. Other characters . . . are more happy-go-lucky and generally 'kid like.' Jazmine and Cindy already show these attributes. It makes a nice balance."

Race remains our great divide, our daily misunderstanding in America. Our comics page contains 20 comics, 19 by white cartoonists. I think there's room for one with a black perspective.

November 30, 2003

Meriden Public Library must clear up this surreal situation

HERE'S WHY MERIDEN Library Director Marcia Trotta can't win in this imbroglio over paintings of Jesus Christ: Her board has adopted contradictory policies.

Meriden's policy on "intellectual freedom" subscribes to the Library Bill of Rights of the American Library Association. It requires that materials for both reading and display be chosen for "the enlightenment of the people of the community" and "not be excluded because of the origin, background, or views of those contributing to their creation." The local policy states specifically, "in no case should library materials be excluded because of the race, nationality or the social, political, or religious views" of the creators of the material.

Paradoxically, the Meriden library's policy on display and exhibit areas requires that art "be appropriate for viewing by all ages" and not "offensive to any segment of the community."

That's impossible.

You can't allow all social, political and religious views and then expect not to offend anyone. It is absurd for any library board member to think they can avoid offending anyone, but to lay that down as law and then claim you believe in intellectual freedom is a mind-bender beyond belief.

Libraries—like the books, magazines, newspapers, films and exhibits they hold within their walls—are bastions of freedom, cradles for creativity, fountains of free thought.

The local Library Board came up with this unworkable formula and revisited it as late as 1999. It ought to untangle it immediately.

The Meriden Library says it "wholly endorses" the Library Bill of Rights, but last week's banishment of religious art violates those rights. "Libraries should challenge censorship" and "cooperate with all persons and groups concerned with resisting abridgment of free expression and free access to ideas," states the Library Bill of Rights.

Even the local provision requiring that exhibits be appropriate for children seems to contradict American Library Association policy, which states: "Denying minors access to certain library materials and services available to adults is a violation of the Library Bill of Rights. Librarians and governing bodies should maintain that parents—and only parents—have the right and the responsibility to restrict the access of their children . . . to library resources."

Not only does the local code contradict national policy, it contradicts itself. Section 3, Paragraph C, states: "No materials will be removed . . . which may be distasteful to certain individuals or groups. No one will be allowed to use his personal prejudices, taste or moral standard to interfere with the free and convenient access to materials."

How does that square with keeping out material "offensive to any segment of the community"? It doesn't. It is an unworkable policy.

Library Board Chairwoman Joan Edgerly should call a special meeting and fix this.

Then local artist Mary Morley should be invited back to exhibit her work. She very rightly cancelled her exhibit after Mrs. Trotta accepted paintings of Moses, Mother Teresa, David and Goliath and others but excluded several paintings of Christ. Under the guidance of these paradoxical policies, she said she felt those paintings would be offensive to some.

Mrs. Trotta is a smart and dedicated public servant and has presided over a fine library and excellent staff. She should lead the way in clearing up this surreal predicament.

No one should worry that this is a church/state constitutional issue. It's not. It is no more unconstitutional to hold a temporary exhibit of religious art in a public space than it is to sing "Silent Night" on the town green.

The local policy takes note of "community standards" in addition to American Library Association policies. Ms. Morley's paintings, like the ones pictured here, do not offend Meriden's community standards.

December 7, 2003

— 2004 —

§ We're all hunting for the truth

THE GREATER PART of the Local & State section front and
the Perspective section front (this page) the past two Sundays
has been taken up with deer hunting. If you've followed it, you
know that the hunter had some squabbles with the writer. It
turns out the writer has some squabbles with the hunter.

My turn.

Hunter Peter Picone and reporter Evan Goodenow are two
honorable men. Mr. Picone has dedicated his life to wildlife.
Mr. Goodenow has dedicated his life to journalism. In his mind,
he got the story right; in Mr. Picone's mind, the story was want-
ing. And perhaps never the twain shall meet.

The two of them and a *Record-Journal* photographer went out
together early one fall morning as Mr. Picone hunted with one
of his sons, one of his favorite things to do. In fact, the story was
about passing the tradition of nature loving and hunting on to
the next generation. Much of Mr. Goodenow's story described
that tradition. Mr. Picone did not think the story went deep
enough and did not like the parts where the reporter quoted a
woman from the Fund for Animals. Last Sunday Mr. Picone
took 1,500 words on this page to set the record straight from his

102

point of view. I said in an editor's note that we felt the original article was fair.

I also agreed with Mr. Picone, a wildlife biologist with the state Department of Environmental Protection and a good source for our staff for years on all things wild in the state, that the article could have been more extensive, and, in fact, that was the original plan. Ah, the best laid plans of mice and men, someone wise once said.

We decided to go with what we had from our time in the woods with the Picones. We had color, detail, dedication and a father and son. But the father bristled and in his piece here last week objected to language by Mr. Goodenow about deer writhing in pain after being hit by an arrow. In his sincere angst over the article, Mr. Picone retorted in print that our reporter "never asked me" about such scenes. Mr. Goodenow, however, did ask the question, and Mr. Picone answered it this way, quoting from Mr. Goodenow's original article: "Picone said most hunters try to kill as humanely as possible and he notes that bears, bobcats and coyote don't concern themselves with how long it takes for their prey to die."

The hunter wrote last week that the reporter "never asked me" about modern bow hunting equipment. Mr. Goodenow, however, called Mr. Picone back to ask him more about his bow and reported in his original article about "razor sharp" arrows the bow could let fly "at up to 300 feet per second."

It was quoting the anti-hunting animal rights activist that really bugged the hunter. Mr. Goodenow wrote that a Fund for Animals spokeswoman "points to a Michigan Department of Natural Resources study" that found 60 percent of deer shot by bow hunters were wounded but not retrieved. The story also pointed out that the Texas wildlife department found it to be 50 percent. These are statistics not from animal rightists, but from wildlife experts in other states.

It would have been good of us to run those numbers by Mr. Picone.

I happen to think that hunting, carried out by knowledge-able people like Mr. Picone, is a noble pursuit. I also think that writing and reporting carried out by knowledgeable people like Mr. Goodenow is a noble pursuit. If there were misunderstand-ings in this process, I hope we have all learned from it.

I appreciate readers who got this far and hope they also read Mr. Goodenow's original story and Mr. Picone's response. I did, and I learned from both.

January 11, 2004

Religion, used as a weapon

IT WAS SOME eighth-graders not long ago who reminded me there are different views of writing. I was telling them about the wonder and power in Ernest Hemingway's *A Farewell to Arms*, what a great storyteller he was and how they should read the book.

A hand shot up and a boy said, "My brother had to read it in English class. He said it was boring."

Then we talked about how people can disagree over books, movies (movies are written before they are filmed), any kind of writing.

Opinion writing—a high art form—invites disagreement. If we all agreed, what a boring planet this would be. What hu-mankind needs to try to do is to get along better even in our disagreements while seeking a more just world. When will we stop going to war and killing each other because some pray to Allah and others pray to Jesus?

A writer can choose to be conciliatory or forceful in getting his message across. I wrote here last that the president panders to our fears and speaks out of both sides of his mouth. He does that about a lot of things, but I was referring to his position on gay marriage.

Sharon Sanders objected. Perhaps you saw her letter last Tuesday stating that I "utterly dismiss the teachings of the Bible," that liberals like me "resort to name calling" and that her point of view "comes from common sense and the Holy Bible."

The column also elicited this from Thomas McMillan, though he disagreed with some of what I wrote: "for only the second time in my life I am responding to a newspaper article/editorial . . . your comments against President Bush were written in a clear and easy-to-understand manner. I respect the way you were . . . able to present your case eloquently and succinctly."

There were others, like the man who wrote, "all you lollypops and other gays get back in the closet (and) start reading the Bible."

There you have it: three different reactions to the same piece of writing. To be sure, I have on occasion called some real lunkheads some names in print, but I didn't last time. And I don't remember "utterly dismissing" the Bible, though I have never been a fan of the part about where a big fish swallowed Jonah, or the parts that defend slavery and the killing of women in case they might be witches.

Now, here's a good part in the good book: "And Ruth said (to Naomi) intreat me not to leave thee, or to return from following after thee: for whither thou goest, I will go; and where thou lodgest, I will lodge: thy people shall be my people, and thy God my God: where thou diest, will I die, and there will I be buried: the Lord do so to me, and more also, if ought but death part thee and me." Ruth 1:16-17.

I can't think of a more beautiful passage about the love of one woman for another. Let the long debate rage over whether it is lesbian love or not.

As I've said before, faith can be a saving force in a society. But too many of us, George Bush sadly in the forefront, are using religion in prejudicial ways to discriminate against gay people, just as narrow religious views were used in the past in this country to commit genocide against Native Americans and to enslave black people.

Mr. McMillan, an African-American, told me that he feels gay-rights activists have unjustly tried to use the civil rights movement to further their cause. But to me, when some people are denied the rights that everyone else has, that is pure and simple discrimination.

To quote Dr. Martin Luther King Jr.: "Injustice anywhere is a threat to justice everywhere."

If he were with us today, he'd have some choice words for the likes of George W. Bush.

February 8, 2004

600,001 daffodils + one CPA

THE DAFFODIL FESTIVAL Committee should change the way it keeps track of the money it collects. According to its own accounting, the 70,000 people attending the festival spent on average $1.70 per person.

Something doesn't add up.

None of the hardworking committee members are allowed near where the cash is counted—$118,736 in ticket sales last year, according to festival records. Only committee chairman Mark Zebora, who is the city's parks and public works director; his mother, two close friends and a cousin of one of those friends who comes from South Carolina each year, count the cash.

The committee should hire a certified public accountant to oversee all financial operations. Committee member Jeffry Cossette, the deputy police chief or his designee, should be there when cash is counted.

Also, counters should be installed at the ticket booths where festivalgoers purchase tickets in $5 books (10 tickets per book). Knowing the number of tickets sold will be a check on the amount of cash counted. There will be no questions about why it comes out to the improbable $1.70 per person. The public will know how many tickets were sold and how much gross revenue that generates. Any respectable CPA would require such a procedure.

Hiring a CPA will also ensure a fuller accounting on required IRS forms and will relieve Mr. Zebora of that burden. He and his committee have done an admirable job of planning and running the city's largest annual event. Turning the financial books over to qualified accountants will ensure public confidence in the integrity of that operation. Also, it is unclear what the city's contribution is, beyond the $20,000 grant. Mr. Zebora estimated, at the newspaper's request, a total of some $65,000 in overtime and other costs. This should be fully documented.

The *Record-Journal* devoted more than a month of reporting, editing and writing on the financial operation of the festival and published a 5,400-word front-page article last Sunday. When we started asking questions about the finances, Mr. Zebora at first refused to provide any answers. We argued that state Freedom of Information laws require disclosure by nonprofits like the Daffodil Festival organization. Similar nonprofits putting on large events, like the Durham Fair, share much more detailed financial information with the public. We eventually received the information we requested. The Daffodil Festival operations should remain an open book for all to see.

We understood we'd be criticized for putting a microscope on the city's signature event, and sure enough, letters about "negative reporting" are rolling in.

The *Record-Journal's* late publisher, Carter H. White, was a founder of the Daffodil Festival. Under his son, Publisher Eliot C. White, the newspaper remains a primary sponsor of the festival, with annual in-kind donations of more than $30,000. Mr.

White and many of his employees volunteer each year at the *Record-Journal* festival booth.

A community newspaper serves its community primarily, however, by shedding light where no light has been shed; by covering news that its editors know they should cover; and by raising questions on issues of public concern to prompt needed reforms. This newspaper would never shirk that responsibility.

The mayor and city councilors are expressing concern and calling for changes. Mr. Zebora said last week that he will form a subcommittee to look into hiring an accountant.

It's time to strengthen the Daffodil Festival by insisting on public accountability.

February 22, 2004

The Scruggs case: Fair trial and free press at odds

The right to a fair trial is . . . essential to the preservation and enjoyment of all other rights, providing a necessary means of safe-guarding personal liberties against government oppression.
 —Supreme Court Justice William J. Brennan

One basic liberty. Freedom of press—the uncontrolled and uncensored exchange in print of ideas, information, arguments, and accusations—is in many ways the essential political liberty. The effective conduct of a free government is dependent upon the existence of a free press; the fortunes of each seem always to rise and fall together.
 —Historian Clinton Rossiter

NOW THAT STATE Superior Court Judge Stephen F. Frazzini has let the guilty verdict stand in deciding that a juror was not biased against Judith Scruggs, she awaits her sentencing.

The Meriden single mother, who works at Super Stop & Shop on East Main Street, was convicted on one count of risk of injury to her 12-year-old son Daniel, who hanged himself in his bedroom closet a little more than two years ago.

Mrs. Scruggs' lawyer, Reese Norris of Hartford, tried to convince the judge that Vincent Giardina III, one of the six jurors in the highly controversial case, was biased against the defendant, based mostly on what he told newspaper reporters.

After subpoenaing Mr. Giardina and two reporters and personally questioning them, Judge Frazzini took the word of the juror over the journalists.

No judge wants his jurors tainted. No judge wants to see a trial he presides over tossed aside as a miscarriage of justice; and this judge, five years into his first term on the bench, would certainly love to keep intact his record of never having been overturned on appeal.

Judge Frazzini (Yale Law School and Yale Divinity School) wrote an impressive, extensively researched—and, in the view of the defense, flawed—18-page decision upholding the integrity of his jury and, implicitly, his court. Judith Scruggs was tried and convicted fairly, he ruled.

From the start, in the judge's own words, this has been "a troubling case." And a complicated one, where twice the issues burgeoned beyond traditional jurisprudence, and our belief that a person is innocent until proven guilty, into a battleground over two conflicting American liberties: fair trial vs. free press.

The free press won the first skirmish after the prosecutor tried to keep the names of the jurors secret.

"Cloaking jurors in anonymity weakens the bond between the juror and the public . . . Dating back to time immemorial, the names of persons serving as jurors have been public knowledge," the judge ruled, and correctly so.

As the trial progressed last fall, the judge threw out one charge against Mrs. Scruggs, the jury found her innocent on two others but guilty on the one count of risk of injury due to a messy home. The press, both local and national, was naturally curious about this: a mother guilty while bullies roam free.

We interviewed four of the six jurors. *60 Minutes* and *Oprah* did segments. All of the Connecticut broadcast outlets were on the scene—West Main Street, with news vans with their TV dishes parked one after another, resembled the front yard of ESPN.

And Stacey Stowe of *The New York Times* wrote on Oct. 12, 2003, a week after the verdict, that juror Giardina "said he supported a conviction, in part, because he did not want Ms. Scruggs to sue the city if she were acquitted."

Rachel Makwana of the *Record-Journal*, who covered more of this case than any other single reporter, asked Mr. Giardina if what he told Stowe was true.

"I would be lying if I said it wasn't," he told Ms. Makwana.

Norris moved for a new trial, claiming juror bias against his client.

Judge Frazzini—the divinity student who decided instead that "my calling was to work for justice," the calm and quiet judge who was equally deferential to each side in this difficult case—must have stomped on his black robes in the privacy of his chambers, or at least wondered if he had charged the jury correctly.

It took more than four months from the publication of the juror's statements to the issuance of his ruling that "the 'extrinsic matter' here, objectively considered, was not of the nature or quality to result in actual prejudice to the defendant's right to a fair trial before an impartial jury."

Norris has promised an appeal, even as Mrs. Scruggs waits to find out how many, if any, of those up to 10 years in jail she faces when Judge Frazzini sentences her on May 14.

It troubled me that he felt compelled to subpoena newspaper reporters doing their jobs. Each newspaper hired legal counsel to fight the subpoenas on First Amendment grounds—that it is an onerous burden to try to do your work of keeping the public informed if you are going to be hauled into court for it.

After losing that argument, the *Record-Journal* and *The New York Times* were successful in arguing that the judge should limit his questioning narrowly to what Mr. Giardina said to Ms. Stowe and Ms. Makwana.

I did not feel the fundamental principle of a free press was damaged by our compelled testimony because it could, I thought, help administer fair justice—a stretch to some, but I saw it as the First Amendment and the Sixth Amendment working in concert on one woman's guilt or innocence.

If a juror did indeed consider "extrinsic" information, like Mrs. Scruggs' plan to sue the city for, among other things, ignoring those who bullied her son, it could be grounds for throwing out the verdict against her and holding a new trial.

Citing case law, though, Judge Frazzini maintained that even if Mr. Giardina did think she shouldn't sue the city, that alone is "not a basis for impeaching the verdict."

The judge chose his words carefully but made it clear his juror did nothing wrong. He wrote that Giardina showed "awareness of his duty to follow the court's admonitions to obey the rules of juror conduct," and stated that he has "observed Giardina testifying on several occasions" and then found, based "on the full array of evidence presented," that there was not "any improper bias or prejudice on this juror's part."

Astute counsel for the press, Daniel Klau of Hartford for the *Record-Journal* and James Rollins of Boston for the *Times*, told me they feel the judge did not question the integrity of their clients, Ms. Makwana and Ms. Stowe.

I am not so sure. Certainly in trying to defend the juror and keep the jury's verdict intact, the judge would have to try to fault the testimony of those who, in essence, showed that the juror changed his tune. All too often, from where I sit, as soon as someone gets into trouble for what they say in print, they start blaming the reporter.

Turning to the sworn testimony of Ms. Stowe of the *Times*, Judge Frazzini wrote in his decision that he "does not find credible the inference drawn by a newspaper reporter" that the juror knew of Mrs. Scruggs' intent to sue as he sat judging her guilt or innocence. He even grasped at her quotation of verb forms in questioning the reporter's "recollection that Giardina used the past-perfect tense."

And after Ms. Makwana testified under oath that Mr. Giardina told her 1) that what he said to Ms. Stowe was true, and 2) that he learned of Mrs. Scruggs' suit "a while ago," the judge maintained that "there is no persuasive evidence" that the juror "actually knew, before the verdict, that the defendant had taken any action to sue the city."

To me it was the juror who was dancing around the truth, not the journalists.

Here are Mr. Giardina's statements since the verdict:

—"Mr. Giardina said he supported a conviction, in part, because he did not want Ms. Scruggs to sue the city if she was acquitted." *The New York Times*, Oct. 12, 2003.

—"When asked Monday if the (*Times*) report were true, Giardina replied, 'I would be lying if I said it wasn't,' adding that he would hate to see Scruggs try to profit from her son's death. He still would have found Scruggs guilty if she had no plans to sue the city, Giardina said." *Record-Journal*, Oct. 14, 2003.

—Scruggs' suit against the city "was mentioned for about 20 seconds on the last day of deliberations when we were pretty much done with the case. It definitely was not on my mind during deliberations." *The Hartford Courant*, Oct. 29, 2003. He said his paraphrased comments in *The Times* were "misrepresented" and "taken out of context."

—"I definitely did not say that," Mr. Giardina said of Ms. Stowe's article—on the witness stand on Oct. 31, under questioning from Judge Frazzini.

—"At no time did I tell her that during deliberations that was on my mind," Giardina said on the witness stand about Ms. Makwana's interview with him.

—He "called and asked if I read (the *Times* story) and said he didn't like the way the article came out. He felt his words were turned against him. He thought they wanted to paint it as if he knew they were going to sue the city," fellow juror Thomas Diaz testified in court on Nov. 14.

Clearly, this is a man who knows how to change his story.

On Dec. 19, 2003, the day Ms. Makwana and Ms. Stowe testified and the judge had thanked them and excused them, he told defense lawyer Norris from the bench, "Ultimately a lot depends on whether or not the court finds the testimony of the reporters credible."

He later said to prosecutor James Dinnan, "If I believe the juror Giardina, and don't believe the reporters, it's pretty easy."

In the end he believed Mr. Giardina, but it wasn't easy.

The reporters were advised to speak the truth and answer the judge's questions directly.

Here is how it went, with slight editing of the transcripts. First Judge Frazzini questioning Ms. Stowe of the *Times*:

FRAZZINI: Now, in the article, one of the paragraphs states, "Mr. Giardina said he supported a conviction, in part, because he did not want Ms. Scruggs to sue the city if she were acquitted." Is that paragraph I read to you an accurate report of what he said to you?

STOWE: Yes, it is.

FRAZZINI: Now, was that the whole of what he said to you on the subject of Ms. Scruggs possibly suing the city?

STOWE: Would you like the direct quote?

FRAZZINI: I would like the direct quote, yes, if you know exactly

STOWE: "I did not want her to sue the Town of Meriden."

FRAZZINI: Do you recall . . . what you said to him that elicited that statement?

STOWE: I asked him what were the reasons he decided

to convict Miss Scruggs ... he repeated it, that statement, once, after saying it. And then he brought it up again in the conversation.

FRAZZINI: When did he bring it up again?

STOWE: Later. And we spoke for probably upwards of 20 minutes. We kept, I kept, circling back to what were the reasons you convicted. And when I would ask, he came up with other reasons beyond that one. But, that came up again.

FRAZZINI: Do you recall the context of the other statements he made to that effect?

STOWE: Well, the first and second time he said it, the statements were virtually back to back. He said it once, and then repeated it, almost staccato-like, 'I did not want her,' you know, immediately after saying it the first time. And then the third time, it was more conversational, in the context of ticking off reasons why he convicted. . . .

FRAZZINI: Did he say anything during the course of your interview with him that either said or suggested that he had information about whether Miss Scruggs had, in fact, taken any steps toward suing the city?

STOWE: I think I recall him saying, "I'd heard that," but not explaining where he had heard it. "I'd heard that she was planning to sue the city." But he didn't say where or how.

FRAZZINI: Did he say anything that would indicate or suggest whether he heard this prior to rendering the verdict?

STOWE: Yes.

FRAZZINI: And what?

STOWE: Yes, that, what indicated it to me was the verb tense that he used when he answered my question. He didn't say, "I do not want her to sue the City of Meriden." He said, "I did not want her." I said, when we were talking about the reasons for his, you know, deciding to convict, he said, "I did not want her to sue the Town of Meriden." So it was the verb tense for me that . . .

FRAZZINI: OK. Now, from that, that sentence to me might

indicate either that he didn't want her to continue on with actions already taken to bring a lawsuit, or to commence the actions to bring a lawsuit. Is there anything else he might have said that would give any indication as to whether or not he knew she'd actually taken some affirmative steps towards bringing a lawsuit?

STOWE: Only that one statement of, "I'd heard that she wanted to sue."

FRAZZINI: And it was, "I had heard."

STOWE: Right.

* * *

The judge next brought Ms. Makwana to the stand and had her sworn in.

FRAZZINI: Now, in the article that you wrote, which is Court's Exhibit Two, the fourth paragraph reads, "When asked Monday if the report were true, Giardina replied, 'I would be lying if I said it wasn't,' adding that he would hate to see Scruggs try to profit from her son's death. He still would have found Scruggs guilty if she had no plans to sue the city, Giardina said." Is that an accurate statement as to what he said?

MAKWANA: Yes, it is.

FRAZZINI: Do you recall what his exact words were? . . .

MAKWANA: I read to him the article, Stacey Stowe's article, the paragraph that says he supported a conviction in part because of her intent to sue the city. I read to him that paragraph word for word, and asked him if that was accurate or if he was misquoted, and he said, "No, I would be lying if I said it wasn't." I mean, "Yes, I would be lying if I said it wasn't."

FRAZZINI: OK. And then, I infer from your article, that he added to that?

MAKWANA: Well, we talked more, had a conversation about the trial and deliberations, and what he knew about her intent to sue. And he had mentioned that he didn't like the fact that she was looking to sue, and didn't like that she was trying to profit from her son's loss. But, also said that he would have found her guilty even if, even if that wasn't the case.

FRAZZINI: OK. What did he tell you about what he knew on this question of the defendant possibly suing?

MAKWANA: He said he had heard about it, and had mentioned it casually during deliberations. And, you know, "Oh, gee, I wonder if she's going to sue?" And that it was quickly dismissed during deliberations and that they moved on.

FRAZZINI: Did he tell you when or how he had heard this?

MAKWANA: No, he didn't know. He didn't know how he had heard it, so he couldn't elaborate.

FRAZZINI: So you asked him?

MAKWANA: I did ask him.

FRAZZINI: Did you ask him when he had heard it?

MAKWANA: Yes.

FRAZZINI: And what did he tell you?

MAKWANA: He said it was a while ago. And that's not word for word, but something to that extent. . . .

FRAZZINI: He told you that he had brought this up in jury deliberations?

MAKWANA: Yes.

FRAZZINI: And that the other jurors had basically hushed him down, or something to that effect?

MAKWANA: Right.

FRAZZINI: Did he tell you whether he, in his own mind, had continued to entertain this as a factor in his own decision?

MAKWANA: No. . . .

FRAZZINI: Did he say anything that would state or suggest to the contrary? Well, let me put it to you, let me make, let me try and make my question simpler. Did he say or, did he say anything that either stated or suggested that her intention to sue figured into his decision to find the defendant guilty, other than what you've already said?

MAKWANA: No . . .

FRAZZINI: So he said to you this was a factor that figured into his decision?

MAKWANA: He said that *The New York Times* paraphrased version of his statements was accurate.

FRAZZINI: And he also told you the other jurors told him he couldn't consider that?

MAKWANA: Right.

FRAZZINI: Did you ask him about any inconsistency between what he told *The New York Times*, that it affected his decision, and the fact that the other jurors told him he couldn't, that they couldn't consider it as a factor?

MAKWANA: Yes.

FRAZZINI: And what did he say on that?

MAKWANA: He said that he realized that and he based, he gave his other reasons for why he found her guilty, and he moved on. And he said, gave me the other reasons for why he found Mrs. Scruggs guilty.

FRAZZINI: Did he say anything to, that would in any way repudiate that he relied on this as a factor?

MAKWANA: No. . . .

FRAZZINI: So during this conversation he told you that he had heard that she intended to file, intended to sue the city?

MAKWANA: It was, right.

FRAZZINI: Is that the way to put it, that he'd heard she intended to sue the city or that he'd heard she had sued the city, do you recall which?

MAKWANA: No, that she was intending to sue the city.

FRAZZINI: And he heard that a while ago?

MAKWANA: A while ago.

FRAZZINI: But he didn't recall where or from whom?

MAKWANA: Right.

FRAZZINI: Did you ever explore with him whether a while ago meant before the deliberations began?

MAKWANA: No, I didn't. . . .

FRAZZINI: Let me see if I, I want to make sure I understand

one thing that you've said, and I'll try and take it in steps again. So he confirmed the accuracy of *The New York Times* article?

MAKWANA: Right.

FRAZZINI: He told you he had heard this information?

MAKWANA: Yes.

FRAZZINI: He told you that he had brought it up during the deliberations, and other jurors told him it couldn't be considered—correct?

MAKWANA: Correct.

FRAZZINI: But he said nothing else that would either state or suggest whether after the other jurors told him it couldn't be considered he, in fact, considered it?

MAKWANA: Right, there was nothing to indicate that.

* * *

These are two professional reporters who covered a trial, interviewed jurors and wrote accurate articles that informed the public on the criminal justice system.

We would like to think that the overwhelming number of citizens who serve on juries do their best to mete out justice. But this "troubling case" makes you wonder. Midway through the trial, Judge Frazzini tossed out the charge against Mrs. Scruggs that her son was at risk of physical harm. The prosecution failed to prove that crime.

The judge was careful to take note over and over that jurors must reach their verdict based only on the evidence presented.

"There was no evidence here that anything in the home environment was likely to injure a child's physical health," Judge Frazzini wrote in a separate decision on March 8, along with his ruling denying a new trial.

But on the day they reached their verdict last fall, jury foreman Thomas Diaz and jurors Paul Kirschmann, Cathleen Hubbard and Mr. Giardina told the *Record-Journal* in separate interviews that their guilty verdict was a direct result of police testimony about the knives in Daniel's closet.

Once again it is the press disclosing to the public how the judicial system worked, or failed to work.

"It's not just that he was sleeping with knives," Diaz told the *Record-Journal.* "She had knowledge that he had the knives and she was OK with that, that he had the knives. And there was a spear. It's not a Swiss Army knife that a kid would have and fold up. These are serrated blades, open blades with no sheath, that he's sleeping with."

All four of these jurors said they found Scruggs guilty as a direct result of police testimony that Daniel slept with knives.

Judge Frazzini, however, wrote: "The only evidence about the safety of the home environment was that Daniel slept near knives and a homemade spear. Although there was evidence that the weapons were found in the closet near Daniel's body, there was no further evidence as to where near his body. There was no evidence whatsoever, either by direct or circumstantial proof, however, that these items or Daniel's use of them was likely to—i.e., would probably—injure either his mental or physical health. There is a difference between sharp implements being potentially unsafe, as many household items may be, and evidence showing that they were kept or used in an unsafe manner that made them likely to injure a child's health."

The portion of the risk-of-injury statute under which Mrs. Scruggs was convicted, the judge said, "prohibits conduct that places a child in a situation that poses a risk of injury to a child's mental health," not physical health.

It's tough being a juror, especially on a difficult case like this one. Ms. Hubbard said she was up all night at times; the case "just consumed you."

But these jurors based their verdict on testimony supporting a criminal charge the judge threw out. I hope they don't all start denying what they said about knives.

Troubling case indeed.

March 21, 2004

Alistair, Humphrey and me

ALISTAIR COOKE KEPT writing until his death at age 95. This erudite expatriate Englishman, this "peerless observer of the American scene" as *The New York Times* put it in his obituary Wednesday, was a prolific journalist and author of more than a dozen books, my favorite his 1977 collection of essays called *Six Men*.

Mr. Cooke wrote of the "one and only" Charles Chaplin, the "tough guy" Humphrey Bogart, the "lord of reason" Bertrand Russell, the audacious and iconoclastic yet "scrupulous correspondent" H.L. Mencken, the "failed saint" Adlai Stevenson and "the golden boy" Edward VIII because he liked them, admired them and all six "made a deep impression" on the 20th century.

His honesty as a writer is what drew me to him. "The simple true answer" on why he chose these men "is that of all the eminent people I have had occasion to run into, these six were the ones who most demonstrably took to me!" His writing resonates because he understands that personal connections can deepen meaning. "They all seem to me to be deeply conservative men, who, for various psychological reasons, yearned to be recognized as hellions or brave progressives. Perhaps that is their real link with this writer."

He called Bogart our first antihero hero. *Casablanca* opened in New York on Thanksgiving Day 1942, two weeks after the Allies invaded North Africa. When Hitler was brutally threatening the world, "Bogart was the only possible antagonist likely to outwit him and survive," wrote Mr. Cooke. The suave Rick in the movie gave us hope when we most needed it.

Maybe Mr. Cooke's Bogart profile talks to me because I know that my grandfather saved Humphrey Bogart's mother's life. The details are lost in family lore, but Maude Humphrey Bogart—a famous children's artist—capsized her boat in a storm on Canandaigua Lake in western New York. The Bogarts had a 55-acre estate on the 17-mile-long lake when my grandfather co-owned a more modest hunting and fishing lodge on the opposite shore. He saw her boat go over in the windblown waves and went to the rescue in his rowboat. He got her safely back to her two-story Victorian "cottage" on Seneca Point.

Steamboats still took the summer people to their private docks. Teenaged Humphrey happily violated lake ordinances by leading his Seneca Point gang to the ships' second decks, then diving into the clear waters of Canandaigua. The young Bogart dove in one day and saved the life of 3-year-old Arthur Hamlin. Several decades later my brother and I bought a small piece of lake property from the aging Mr. Hamlin a mile down from our grandfather's lodge.

A decade after *Casablanca*, when Stevenson was running for president against Eisenhower in the era of McCarthy's anti-Communist witch hunts, Bogart flew to Washington to defend the right of several subpoenaed Hollywood colleagues to think and say "anything they damn please."

It was "murmured around the (studio) lots that an open embrace of Stevenson might possibly weaken the bonds of a film contract, there was a glad rush of stars all too eager to be seen liking Ike," wrote Mr. Cooke. "Bogart and his wife (Lauren Bacall) packed their bags and went off with Stevenson."

That same year my grandfather's youngest daughter, my mother, handed out Stevenson buttons.

To Alistair Cooke, Bogart was "a man with a tough shell hiding a fine core." Stevenson had "something more splendid, in a public man, than a record of power. It was simply an impression of goodness." He and the others in this book "left a lasting impression by the energy of their idealism."

They are all dead and gone, but we have Alistair Cooke's words for always.

April 4, 2004

⅜ Eyes on the prize

A PEEK INSIDE the Pulitzer process

Hardly a year goes by that there isn't some controversy over the Pulitzer Prizes, partly because the stakes are so high over American journalism's most prestigious award.

The Pulitzer Prize board decided not to pick a winner for feature writing after the editors on the jury spent three intensive days winnowing down some 150 entries to three finalists.

The board also rejected the jury recommendations for public service, including the *Providence Journal's* incredible yearlong coverage on the causes and consequences of the West Warwick, R.I., nightclub fire where 100 people perished, in favor of *New York Times* reporting on deaths in American factories.

The all-powerful, 19-member board moved the *Times'* entry from a different category into Public Service to the chagrin of the finalists and the jurors for Public Service reporting. The board is chaired by Lee C. Bollinger, president of Columbia University, which under the will of Joseph Pulitzer administers the Pulitzers.

The university and the board invite journalists to be jurors and tell them in advance that, though it is rare, the board might change the selections of the nominating juries in the 14 journalism award categories.

I was one of seven jurors for commentary writing and am satisfied, even proud, of the way the judging went for the nearly 200 writers who sent in the required 10 columns and hoped to win the Pulitzer. To say it was hard to choose three is to say it is hard to get half a dozen gardeners to agree on which is more beautiful, a red or a yellow rose.

Now some roses droop without enough sun, or stunt without enough water, and it is true that not all columnists are born equal or get the care and feeding others get. But each writer had to be read by at least four jurors. Our jury chairman was Keith Woods of the Poynter Institute, the journalism think-tank and career development center in St. Petersburg, Fla. He wrote in his column at *Poynter.org* last week that entrants "got a good read whether you worked for a paper in the smallest market or the largest, whether you'd clipped some stories and sent them in yourself or you got one of those glossy portfolios that came with the backing of the executive editor."

It felt good to read such a rich load of thoughtful commentary from all over this country. By the end of our first day of judging in a large, high-ceilinged room on the Columbia campus, we still had a hundred columnists to consider.

Writers didn't make it, to quote Mr. Woods, if they were "boring, dull or corny; fond of cliches; a fan of quoting (themselves); glib, smug or flippant; or given to writing feature stories."

We looked for writers with a strong voice, a distinct point of view, who displayed clarity of thought and managed to also acknowledge opposing points of view, even if it is a device to castigate that view. To some of us, fairness was important—though I wrestle with that because I'm not sure an opinion needs to be, or even can be, fair.

But our judging was. If someone from your newspaper was under consideration, you had to leave the room for the discussion on that writer. *New York Daily News* executive editor Michael Goodwin left when we debated the merits of his sports columnist Mike Lupica, who fell late on the second day of judging.

It bothered me to see Nat Hentoff of the Village Voice go down before he even got to me. If there is a constitutional scholar among the fraternity of opinion scribes, it is Mr. Hentoff. His colleague Sydney H. Schanberg, whose coverage of the genocide in Cambodia won a Pulitzer in 1976 and spawned the movie *The Killing Fields*, also fell to some lesser-known voices this year.

It got harder and harder and our debates intensified. Mr. Woods was good at keeping discussion focused and civil. We came from Ohio, New York, California, Florida and Connecticut, from papers large and small. Our final seven included writers from Washington, Little Rock, Ark., St. Louis and San Francisco. In the end we picked Nicholas Kristof of the *New York Times* (my first choice), Cynthia Tucker of the *Atlanta Journal-Constitution* and Leonard Pitts of the *Miami Herald*.

The board awarded the Pulitzer to the 46-year-old Mr. Pitts for writing with "passion and compassion (in) vibrant prose that often lands like a punch to the gut."

Mr. Kristof takes up causes of the downtrodden in places on earth where no one else goes. His courage is boundless. But I do not argue with the choice of Leonard Pitts.

April 11, 2004

Even on the right, it's wrong

NO, I AM not Glenn Richter, the fellow who usually occupies this space. He took last week off, but he holds forth some 50 weeks a year, year after year in this corner.

He writes his vapid invective—er, I mean composes his award-winning prose—with such awesome regularity, it seems odd, doesn't it, not to find him here. The last time he was absent, we published someone else with a little note from Glenn that he was resting—that's his inborn humor at work.

I thought I might try to share some of our back-and-forth, since he is always here on the right and I am over there on the left, when Jacqueline Smith isn't. He likes to think it takes two liberals to equal his powerful conservative-libertarian mind.

Every once in a while, he will wander into my office and tell me how hard it is to write stuff because he's a lonely voice over here on the right in this newspaper. I scoff and remind him to look inside on the op-ed page at Lowry and Safire and Jacoby, the home of syndicated scribes of Mr. Richter's bent, not to forget Kathleen Parker, who every once in a while makes an appearance in this paper.

I was judging opinion writers vying for the Pulitzer Prize recently and was pushing Ms. Parker, not because I agree with much of what she has to say, but she is able to say it well and with humor—my God a right-winger with humor! Alas, she did not win.

Glenn and I were discussing the war in Iraq (he's for it, I'm not), and he had to agree with me that President Bush lied to the people. "But so did Johnson lie about Vietnam," he rejoined.

"Johnson was right about civil rights and wrong about the war," I responded. "Yes, he lied about Vietnam, just like Nixon lied about Vietnam."

"And Clinton lied about . . ."

"Yes, about that," I agreed.

So I've thought about lying about having oral sex in the Oval Office and lying about war. And then I thought about those who supported President Clinton and his policies being disappointed in him for his trysts with Monica and then not telling the truth.

I wondered why those who support President Bush don't express more disappointment in his lies.

I think it is because those who like Bush like his war too, no matter that Iraq had nothing to do with 9/11 or terrorism before we invaded—that was the big lie from Bush and his administration that so many bought and still buy—that Saddam Hussein was a terrorist sending Al Qaeda's terror to our shores. Wasn't true any more than the weapons of mass destruction are true.

Johnson and Nixon kept telling us we were keeping all of Southeast Asia from going communist. What we were doing was shoring up a corrupt South Vietnamese regime that wouldn't have held up more than a minute without our half a million troops in the country.

When we left, none of the famous dominoes fell. Nearly

60,000 Americans and somewhere between 2 million and 3 million Vietnamese were killed. What for? I ask. What is honorable about dying for a lie?

Mr. Richter has argued eloquently and ferociously that it was a good thing the monster Saddam was dethroned. OK, I say, but what about all the other monsters out there all over the world?

Powerful men who send American soldiers off to die for the wrong reasons should lose their power.

Johnson lost his job over Vietnam. Nixon lost his over other lies.

Now it is Bush's turn. Another war, more lying to the American people. We'll see if the voters put up with it come November.

And Mr. Richter should be back next week to set us all straight.

May 16, 2004

Author can be unbiased as reporter

FORMER MALONEY HIGH football coach Rob Szymaszek and his wife Diane are friends with me and my wife Jacky. Assistant Sports Editor Bryant Carpenter is writing a book with Mr. Szymaszek about his battle with brain cancer.

None of the above affects in any way our coverage of sports and in particular the coverage of a growing rift between Wayne Flis, who just lost the head football coaching job at Maloney, and Mr. Szymaszek. We report today that both men are applying for the job and that supporters of Mr. Flis say Mr. Szymaszek undermined him in order to get the job back for himself. There are two sides to the story and we report both sides as well as we can, as we should.

Some have told us they believe Mr. Carpenter has a conflict because he is writing a book. He doesn't.

Reporter Dan Champagne wrote today's story. Mr. Carpenter contributed to it.

Anyone who knows Bryant Carpenter knows he is an honest man and an honest journalist. As best he can—and his best has been on display here for more than a decade—he writes fair and compelling journalism. It is common practice for journalists to write books, honest books. I'm sure Mr. Carpenter and Mr. Szymaszek will write a fascinating account of a football coach benched by brain cancer. We are hopeful the story will find a publisher and that people in Meriden and beyond will read it. Writing a book does not compromise a journalist. It enhances his knowledge and his credibility.

When Bob Woodward of *The Washington Post* wrote books on President Bush, partisans may think he became a shill for the president, but in fact, though he was on leave to do the books, he continued to contribute to the *Post's* coverage of the Bush White House. He helped his newspaper's coverage in all that he learned while doing the book. I know that Mr. Woodward himself did not feel at all compromised. The Pulitzer Prize winner, who gained fame by uncovering Watergate with Carl Bernstein, has been called the best reporter of his generation.

Bryant Carpenter has the same integrity. He knows Wayne Flis, he knows Rob Szymaszek. He has always been professional with both.

It was months ago that we planned the book project with Mr. Szymaszek. Our assistant sports editor went on the special assignment virtually as Mr. Flis was disciplined and removed from his coaching position for, it appears, swearing at a student. Mr. Carpenter knows as much about Maloney football as anyone on our staff and so Sports Editor Bob Morrissette told him he needs to contribute to our reporting. I agree with that decision.

Though some people will use anything they can to charge bias in the media, I know that this newspaper can cover this issue with absolute fairness and with a fervent desire to get to the truth. That's what we do day in and day out—try to get to the truth.

Rob Szymaszek is my friend. Today we are publishing a story highly critical of him. My friendship would not and did not and will not get in the way of truthful and honest journalism. I've known him only since his operation. We disagree, we have found, on just about everything, from war and peace to football and soccer, soccer being the better game.

We have both acknowledged to each other that friendship means there are times when we must understand our chosen professions come first. He has told me there are confidences he must keep about his school that he knows I would like to know about. And I have told him things will appear in this newspaper that he would prefer not be reported.

He knows and everyone else should know that we are committed to our very souls to report the truth to our readers.

June 18, 2004

Just like telling a friend

AS A YOUNG reporter, I'd stare at the blank white sheet of paper in my manual typewriter and ponder which words to choose to tell my story.

Good writing has its rules just as good carpentry, good engineering, good cooking—too much salt, too little butter and you've spoiled the pie. Pick the wrong verb, the wrong noun, head down the wrong path and you're off on a tangent. You've lost your way. The story fizzles. The reader gives up.

We'd ask each other, we reporters sitting at desks in rows in the large warehouse of a newsroom—before we'd walk the multiple sheets of double-spaced prose up to our editors—we'd ask each other if the words were working. In news writing, the "lede"—the first paragraph or two—is important. We'd ask each other if the ledes worked, if the quote fit.

Beginnings and endings are important to any story. Feature stories are different than news stories, and judging whether they are good or not is harder than seeing whether you have written an effective news article. Laboring over features, perhaps a profile of a person or describing a trip down a river in a canoe, we'd get a little philosophical with each other right there in the pumped-up atmosphere of the newsroom.

"Who are you writing for?" someone would ask.

"All our readers," someone would answer.

Someone else would say, "No way; not all our readers are interested in canoes or rivers."

"It's our job to make them interested," someone else would offer.

"Not really; clearly some of our stories are for only some of our readers," the poor guy saddled with the state utilities beat would say.

But it is important to know who your audience is, our editors would remind us.

"I don't write to please anyone. I write to please myself. I make demands on myself. Am I satisfied with what I wrote?" I remember one of the best writers at the paper saying. I think he compared it to playing golf as opposed to baseball. In one game you are part of a team, in the other you are on your own, competing against yourself.

What he said reminded me of the best advice I ever got on writing: write the story as if you are writing a letter to a good friend. An audience of one. You want your best friend to understand what you are trying to say, you want the friend to keep reading to the end.

Every reporter, every writer needs to find his or her own way. What works best for them in putting one sentence after another. We have our ethics and our rules—fairness, balance, truth, accuracy. Those are good guides. They are the frame for a creative process at a daily newspaper that can take place in 600 words written in 20 minutes late at night just before last deadline; or in several weeks or even months on a major project where thousands of words will be written and rewritten and tested and edited without daily deadline pressure. Both forms take skill and knowledge.

Whether we are presenting coverage of the war in Iraq, the Bush–Kerry campaign, or writing about whether two young girls can keep their two pygmy goats or not, remember there is a writer behind every story trying to pick the right words, to the tell the story as compellingly as he or she can.

The decisions in reporting and writing are neither political, nor liberal, nor conservative, nor a formula from the latest marketing studies. It is hard and lonely work, even in the midst of a chaotic newsroom. Putting one word after another is a task like no other, except maybe an artist facing a blank canvas. A writer starts with a blank sheet of paper, or blank computer screen. At the end you have communicated, you have reached someone. Then it is on to the next story.

June 27, 2004

More of us seem to 'get it' about the First Amendment

LIBRARIES AND NEWSPAPERS are buddies. They are guardians together of intellectual freedom, free speech—or, more expansively, free expression. American libraries and newspapers are the first place to go for citizens seeking support for the First Amendment.

That is why it is so heartening to see the Meriden Library Board in the process of changing an old policy that curiously did not uphold the principles of free expression and caused a furor last December when the library rejected certain paintings of Jesus by local artist Mary Morley.

This newspaper and several of its columnists, including me, called for a change in the rules. I can't remember when an issue caused so many letters to the editor. The people overwhelmingly challenged the library over its perceived censorship. Banning Jesus at Christmastime, though done under the board's policy, rankled a whole lot of people.

That policy read in part, and still does until the board formally votes on the proposed changes, "The library will not accept exhibits which are judged *inappropriate* or *offensive* (my emphasis) to any segment of the community." I said then and still say you simply can't put up artwork that won't offend somebody.

The local exhibit policy contradicted the broader library selection policy. The selection policy adheres closely to the American Library Association's Library Bill of Rights, which prohibits removal of materials that "may be distasteful to certain individuals or groups."

The ALA's Bill of Rights is an inspiring document for any freedom-loving people. It echoes the First Amendment of the Bill of Rights adopted by the Founding Fathers in 1791.

Freedom of speech (including painting) was written into our Constitution to protect expression that many, even the majority sometimes, would rather ban. Supreme Court Justice Oliver Wendell Holmes Jr. put it eloquently in 1919: "The best test of truth is the power of the thought to get itself accepted in the competition of the market. . . . we should be eternally vigilant against attempts to check the expression of opinions that we loathe."

The ALA Bill of Rights states bluntly: "Libraries should challenge censorship . . . librarians have a professional responsibility to be inclusive, not exclusive." And this wonderful passage (Section 53.1.12): "The American Library Association believes that freedom of expression is an inalienable human right, necessary to self-government, vital to the resistance of oppression, and crucial to the cause of justice."

It was library director Marcia Trotta who took the brunt of the criticism for deciding to leave out some of Ms. Morley's paintings while accepting others, but she made that decision under the misguided policy of trying not to offend anyone. She felt some of the depictions of Jesus would be regarded as offensive.

Her staff wrote a letter to the editor expressing its "unwavering faith" in Ms. Trotta's judgment. The 25 employees went on that they were "appalled by the slanted and sensationalized 'news' coverage presented by both print and electronic media and are amazed by the hatefully crude, insulting and abusive calls, letters and comments made to her by concerned citizenry. Marcia has served this community faithfully, compassionately and never less than professionally for over 30 years."

It says a lot when everyone on the staff publicly supports the boss. I agree that Marcia Trotta always has been highly professional, but I disagreed with the policy she was working under and with the idea that this newspaper's news coverage was slanted. It wasn't. Each article elucidated all sides of the controversy. The opinion columns, which are not news articles, were clearly labeled commentary, and a newspaper without local columnists is not much more than a bland collection of newsprint pages.

I had hoped that a staff of librarians, in supporting their boss, would publicly support the precepts of the Library Bill of Rights as well as the newspaper's right to publish and the people's right to speak out on issues of public importance. After all, the library staffers were exercising their First Amendment rights in sending their letter to the editor.

The episode is evidence of just how frail our inalienable rights can be when even librarians rail against those who are exercising their right to free expression.

But now the library board is heading in the right direction. In the three-page new policy draft there is not one reference to art that may offend. In fact, it emphasizes that art exhibits should "broaden horizons" and "nourish intellectual, aesthetic and creative growth."

Library Board chairman Joan Edgerly told me last week that board members have worked long and hard to come up with a better policy. She was also reassuring that the Meriden Library holds fast to the ALA Bill of Rights. The draft policy still must be vetted by the city corporation counsel's office, but Ms. Edgerly says she is happy with what they have written and expects it to be adopted soon.

The policy comes when an appreciation of the First Amendment is on an upswing in the country.

The First Amendment Center and the American Journalism Review just announced that Americans' support for First Amendment freedoms—shaken by the 9/11 terrorist attacks—is rebounding.

Its annual State of the First Amendment survey, conducted by the University of Connecticut, found that just 30 percent of those surveyed agreed with the statement: "The First Amendment goes too far in the rights it guarantees," with 65 percent disagreeing. The nation was split evenly, 49 percent to 49 percent, on that same question two years ago.

It often happens, sadly, in times of national emergency that overzealous legislators and people seeking safety before liberty endanger our basic rights. So it is troubling that nearly one-third of the survey respondents believe the First Amendment grants too much freedom, but encouraging that the vast majority support it.

Not all is rosy, however, to those of us who cherish the First Amendment. The survey showed that very few could name all five freedoms and only 1 percent of Americans could name "the right to petition the government for redress of grievances"— in other words, it is OK to tell the government you don't like what it is doing. Most, 58 percent, knew free speech is one of the protected rights, but only 17 percent could name freedom of religion, 10 percent knew the right to peaceable assembly, and 15 percent got that a free press is protected by the First Amendment.

When 85 percent can't identify freedom of the press, then you begin to understand this statistic: 49 percent of the survey respondents think the media has too much freedom to publish whatever it wants (while 34 percent feel there is too much government censorship).

When I speak in schools—even to seniors in high schools, even to journalism majors in college—and emphasize that in this country we can think, speak and write what we please, it amazes me that many students get anxious and nervous about that. I worry that our schools are not teaching about our freedoms. And the survey bears out those doubts.

Just 28 percent rated America's education system as doing an "excellent" or "good" job of teaching students about First Amendment freedoms.

That is why newspapers must inform our citizens, as this column is attempting to do. History teachers need to stop droning on about the Bill of Rights and find exciting and creative ways for young Americans to understand "liberty and justice for all." Schools must teach about basic American rights, and libraries must practice First Amendment rights.

The annual survey has been conducted since 1997 examining public attitudes toward freedom of speech, press and religion and the rights of assembly and petition. This year it was conducted nationally by telephone with 1,000 respondents between May 6 and June 6. The sampling error is plus or minus 3 percentage points.

Copies of all of the survey, along with commentaries and analysis, are available on the Web at http:www.firstamendmentcenter.org/sofa_reports/index.aspx. Printed copies of the survey can be obtained from the First Amendment Center, with a written request to: "2004 State of the First Amendment," First Amendment Center, Vanderbilt University, 1207 18th Avenue South, Nashville, TN 37212.

July 11, 2004

§ 'Negative'? How about 'truthful'?

IT WAS ONLY a few sentences in an 83-page report on economic development in Meriden. Given that it is about the press, the sentiments of some survey respondents are not surprising.

"The presence of a strong local media was mentioned as both a strength and weakness of the city. It is an obvious strength, as there is more news and information about the city and the region. However, some interviewees expressed the opinion that the negative reporting portrayed the city poorly." (Page 82, *Meriden Analysis 2004*, by the Connecticut Economic Resource Center.)

I like the ring of "strong local media" and I'm sure the reference to "negative reporting" isn't about the *International Herald Tribune's* coverage of our city. When you are talking about the economic life of a community, what should a local newspaper do?

One thing it shouldn't do is wear rose-colored glasses or bend the news to fit someone's perceptions of "good news." At one neighboring newspaper not long ago, the publisher told the editor to assign a story about the good retail climate at Christmastime. The editor knew buying was off, retails sales were down. The publisher still ordered good news only. The editor quit. He works here now. We don't fabricate news.

A community newspaper needs to reflect the community back to itself. It needs to help the community talk with itself. It needs to cover all the news, good and bad. It is often in the eye of the beholder, though, isn't it? Platt beats Maloney 14–7. Good news for Platt, but what about Maloney?

Sometimes it is obvious: downtown flooded, gang wars at Mills apartments, city manager imprisoned for corruption. All that was true a decade ago. The city's reputation was at its nadir. It was all bad news, covered extensively in this newspaper.

But were there silver linings? A flood commission was established and has been working to solve the ages-old problem. Gang leaders were jailed and gangs diminished. An honest city manager was hired. A grassroots organization called Community Vision organized and worked on various projects for the betterment of the city. All of that, too, was covered extensively in this newspaper.

Reporters and editors don't really think in terms of negative reporting or positive reporting. We think in terms of accurate storytelling. We try to be fair to the people and the issues we cover.

Downtown Meriden is not a pretty sight with its shuttered buildings. We know. We're downtown; have been since 1867. Compare downtown Meriden to, say, downtown Middletown—Meriden has a long way to go.

That doesn't mean good things haven't happened. A new YMCA opened. We covered it. A new local bank, Castle Bank, opened. We covered it. A new community theater opened, Castle Craig Players. We covered it. A library bookstore opened. We covered it.

Every new good thing that happens, we cover it. We should, we want to, we do.

A couple of Sundays ago, we interviewed and wrote about and took pictures of hookers plying their trade on East Main Street in broad daylight. Negative reporting? How about truthful reporting.

We believe problems can't be tackled if no one knows about them.

The economic-development report, which cost the city $18,000, has been generally well received and the survey got a good 19 percent response—243 of more than 1,200 businesses contacted. In fact, only 15 respondents complained about negative newspaper reporting. I like to think that means that the vast majority sees their local paper providing citizens with the news they need to make informed decisions.

August 15, 2004

Let's put Rathergate in context

CALLS FOR CBS News anchor Dan Rather's head are premature. He made a mistake by airing and defending what appear to be bogus documents about President Bush's National Guard service.

Mr. Rather and CBS News, as all news organizations should, acknowledged the error. CBS has appointed two men, a former attorney general and the retired president of the Associated Press, to investigate what went wrong and to make a public report on their findings. Until then, no one should be fired.

I have never been a big fan of Dan Rather, though it is indisputable he has had a distinguished career dating back to his coverage of John F. Kennedy's assassination. I've always thought Walter Cronkite and David Brinkley were better journalists. They set the standard. No one in broadcast journalism has risen to their level.

Mr. Rather, it seems to me, made two mistakes—going with just one source against the unwritten rule of at least two sources, especially on controversial stories; and rushing the story when CBS's own experts questioned the authenticity of the documents. Further, Mary Mapes, the producer on the story (producers are reporters who do much of the research and interviewing), put their source in touch with the Kerry campaign, in violation of network news standards of staying clear "of any political agenda," said CBS.

The man who gave CBS the documents asked, perhaps made it a condition of releasing them, for telephone access to a high-level Kerry campaign official. Senior Kerry aide Joe Lockhart subsequently had a three-minute phone call with the source, apparently about Vietnam as an issue, not about the documents.

The Bush campaign has called for Kerry to "come clean" about the relationships between his campaign and the CBS *60 Minutes* story. Frankly, I'd rather see the president come clean on why he stopped flying and explain the gaps in his service. To me, that's more important than whether or not a TV reporter asked a political operative to make a phone call.

Reporters deal with competing politicians and their supporters all the time. Trading information is not unusual in covering politicians. Our ethics code in the manual we hand out to every reporter, photographer and editor, states: "The newspaper should strive for impartial treatment of issues and dispassionate handling of controversial subjects. . . . Staff should be free of obligations to news sources and newsmakers."

So a guy comes to me with what he says are authentic documents proving the president got preferential treatment in the National Guard, which helped him avoid serving in Vietnam. I can have the documents if I'll help put the source in touch with a top Kerry aide.

Is that an obligation I should avoid? Am I staying impartial by asking Joe Lockhart to call my source? CBS has already said it violates its rules. Retired AP President Lou Boccardi and former Attorney General Richard Thornburgh may answer that. (Mr. Thornburgh is an odd choice by CBS, since he worked for George H. W. Bush).

I'm not sure asking someone to make a phone call is such a huge breach of ethics. But I might say to the source, "Once the story is public, I'm sure Kerry's people would like to talk to you and you don't need me to be your intermediary." The true journalistic obligation is to contact the other side, in this case President Bush, and offer the opportunity to respond, which CBS did.

More fundamentally—make sure those documents are real before you print or air the story. That's where CBS went astray. It was a mistake, but I'm not sure it's a career-ending mistake.

September 26, 2004

Freedom: Limit it and we lose it

PRESS BASHING HAS reached a crescendo, mostly from ideologues from both the left and the right who thought coverage was skewed against them. Those of us in the storytelling craft have grown thick skins, but it gets tiring to hear so often of our faults, of which we have many.

I don't think bias is one of them. The editors I know try hard to print the truth and fight through the spin of feuding politicians. We in the press make the mistake of letting others define us or try to define us—everyone from Rush Limbaugh, who never had to write 600 words on deadline, to Michael Moore, who sees an establishment bias in mainstream media.

What goes missing too often is that a free press represents a free people. Efforts to thwart free reporting are really efforts to thwart the people's right to know.

My friend and colleague Joel Rawson, the smart and feisty editor of *The Providence Journal*, offers some thoughts on this page about recent assaults on freedom of the press. Reporting is, he says, "the freedom of one citizen to talk to another without fearing the government. It is the freedom to listen as well as to speak. It is the right of free inquiry."

Americans should listen to the Joel Rawsons of our society far more than to the loud and obnoxious talk radio screamers who barely comprehend the meaning of the word inquiry.

A free press was founded at the birth of our country as a check on power, and it should be alarming to Americans when the government goes after reporters for doing their jobs. We have gone beyond press bashing to press prosecutions—as recently as Thursday, when a Rhode Island television reporter was found in contempt of court for refusing to divulge his sources.

The government argues that all citizens have a duty to testify in a court of law. But forcing reporters to divulge who gave them information not only exposes the confidant to danger; it requires a reporter to break a promise made in good faith. Consider that a journalist is already doing public duty by writing the news. Democracy works only with an informed public.

A federal judge in Rhode Island wants to know who leaked a surveillance tape of bribe-taking to television reporter Jim Taricani. Taricani refuses to say, and now faces six months in jail.

The New England Society of Newspaper Editors issued a statement Friday decrying the action as "an act of judicial intimidation against a news reporter and assault on the First Amendment and its assurance of a free press. . . . All citizens concerned with the erosion of their First Amendment rights (should) work toward ensuring that no one has to see this type of harassment against our free press again."

NESNE has called for a federal shield law to protect reporters' sources. Sen. Christopher Dodd, D-Conn., introduced federal legislation Friday to do just that.

The Free Speech Protection Act of 2004 would establish a reporters' shield law modeled after laws in 31 states and the District of Columbia.

"This legislation is fundamentally about good government and the free and unfettered flow of information to the public," said Dodd. "The American people deserve access to a wide array of views so that they can make informed decisions and effectively participate in matters of public concern. When the public's right to know is threatened, and when the rights of free speech and free press are at risk, all of the other liberties we hold dear are endangered."

Mr. Taricani has this on his office wall from Thomas Jefferson: "Our liberty depends on freedom of the press, and that cannot be limited, without being lost."

November 21, 2004

Free press is under attack

WE APPRECIATE OUR letter writers. They enliven our pages and make for a vibrant public dialogue, which is what democracy is all about.

George Stowell of Wallingford wrote last week that he agrees with me "that the press must be able to operate free of any government interference." We rarely agree. But he ruined my pleasant surprise by going on, with some flair, about his perception of a liberal bias in the media, Dan Rather being Exhibit 1.

Mr. Stowell's well-written but erring letter is a prime example of a dangerous trend—people who disagree with the news claiming it is biased. Over the many years of listening to reader complaints, I've concluded that more and more of them are from an ideological point of view. People can't stand to read something that doesn't fit their opinions. (That's why so many conservatives are tuning in to Fox news, a biased network that ought to admit it.) Conservatives find a comfort zone with Fox.

But news ought not to be comforting. It ought to inform, reveal, and explain the challenges we face, and it ought to do this fairly and accurately.

Mr. Stowell and I agree that Mr. Rather's *60 Minutes* piece on George Bush's Air National Guard service was flawed. CBS acknowledged the documents they received had not been authenticated and apologized.

But where Mr. Stowell goes awry is thinking that Mr. Rather was practicing some kind of liberal bias by going after the story. Why can't viewers see news coverage, flawed though it may be, as an attempt to get at the truth? That's what a free press does: pursues the truth and tries to keep government honest.

Officials at all levels often try to hide the truth or spin it to their advantage, thus skewing what is true. CBS let the public down on this story, not even bothering to get a second source and their only source turned out to be untrustworthy. But what news organization wouldn't try to find out what happened with George Bush when he was in the National Guard? President Bush, of course, could clear it all up by answering a few questions, which he refuses to do. Why did you stop flying? Why didn't you take your physical? Why did you stop showing up for duty? And then he has the gall to land on an aircraft carrier claiming victory in Iraq.

We may never know about the gaps in his service. There are those who don't care. But I always care when a high public official—especially the president, Republican or Democrat—refuses to answer questions.

This crescendo of complaint against the press should have more of us worried. It has been a constant drumbeat from the blowhards on AM talk radio, nearly all from the right, for years now. Men (mostly) who don't have a clue how to write a fair and balanced story.

The bad wind is blowing harder. Prosecutors and judges are threatening reporters with jail if they don't cough up their sources. The governor of Maryland has ordered his commissioners not to talk to a *Baltimore Sun* reporter and columnist because he doesn't like the way they write. The president worships secrecy to an unhealthy degree in a democracy—even ordering that historical documents from the Reagan-Bush I era be kept from researchers when they should by law be public.

We are "endowed by our creator" with certain "unalienable" rights. The right to know, the right to ask. Americans should be more concerned about the high-decibel criticism of the press morphing into the loss of our rights of free speech and free press. The U.S. Constitution secured the "blessings of liberty to ourselves and our posterity." I worry today about us and our posterity.

December 5, 2004

— 2005 —

§ The 'wall of separation' is real

AFTER I QUOTED Thomas Jefferson's famous letter to the Danbury Baptists about how the American people built "a wall of separation between Church & State," one of our regular letter writers responded that I was perpetuating myths and "there is no wall of separation between church and state in the constitution."

Well, how about this: "The First Amendment has erected a wall between church and state. That wall must be kept high and impregnable."—U.S. Supreme Court Justice Hugo Black, 1947.

I love the dialogue between the newspaper and the readers, and opinions differ, but surely we must agree on some basic facts of American life.

But let's back up. The Founders packed five freedoms into the First Amendment to the Constitution: freedom of religion, speech, press, the rights to peaceable assembly and to petition the government (to tell the government it is wrong).

The part about religion has confused us ever since 1791, when the Bill of Rights was adopted. "Congress shall make no law respecting an establishment of religion, or prohibiting the free exercise thereof," is how it reads. It is good to remember that the Founders were revolutionaries—they changed the world.

One of the biggest changes they made, and Jefferson was in the forefront, was to ban official religions.

Since Plymouth Rock, the colonists escaped religious persecution in Europe but continued it in the New World. If you didn't submit to Puritanism, you couldn't live in Massachusetts Bay. That's why Roger Williams and Ann Hutchinson moved to (fled to) Rhode Island, where they could worship as they pleased.

A century later, Jefferson argued to keep government out of religion. In his native Virginia, he pointed out, it was still legal to burn a heretic to death. "Millions of innocent men, women and children since the introduction of Christianity, have been burnt, tortured, fined and imprisoned," he argued.

Both he and Benjamin Franklin, though declaring Christianity the best religion "the world ever saw," questioned Jesus' divinity (as most of the world's people do today). It's not, however, about which religion is the best. Religion is, in Jefferson's words, "a matter which lies solely between Man & his God."

In writing the majority opinion in 1947 (*Everson v. Board of Education*), Justice Black put it this way: "The 'Establishment of religion' clause of the First Amendment means at least this: Neither a state nor the federal government can set up a church. Neither can pass laws which aid one religion, aid all religions, or prefer one religion over another. Neither can force nor influence a person to go to or to remain away from church against his will or force him to profess a belief or disbelief in any religion . . . No tax in any amount, large or small, can be levied to support any religious activities or institutions."

That's why school officials cannot require students to pray. The Everson decision approved transporting students to parochial schools on public school buses because it was seen as a general benefit to the students, not a religious requirement. A town council or Congress can have chaplains start a session with prayer because there is no compulsion such as there is in the required attendance in a school classroom.

Most American political leaders are grounded in some form of spirituality. The Founders were sure to add the "free exercise" clause—we can believe what we want, but more importantly no one can force us to adopt their set of beliefs. A school cannot force a Jewish student or anyone else to say the Lord's Prayer. Individuals can be religious or not. That is freedom. That is the American way.

January 30, 2005

⸿ Too much freedom? Hardly.

HALF OF AMERICAN high school students think the First Amendment goes "too far" in the freedoms it guarantees. Who is teaching these kids? We all are, and we have to do better.

Roughly half the more than 100,000 students polled by University of Connecticut researchers also wrongly believed the U.S. government has the right to censor the Internet, and half think it's OK for the government to approve newspaper stories before they are printed. The government can't do that.

I've written before that when I speak in high schools and colleges and emphasize how in this country we can think, speak and write what we please, many students get anxious and nervous. It's clear they haven't grasped the importance of our basic freedoms.

There are other sad examples of sending the wrong message to our youth. In Meriden, after more than a year since a controversy over paintings of Christ, the library still can't decide how to display the works of local artists. In Cheshire, a band of angry Catholics tried to get the town government to shut down a play based on "Romeo and Juliet."

If painters can't display their creative works, and actors can't act, what have we come to? Why would teenagers around here think America guarantees freedom of expression when the library, of all places, prevents it, and parents are clamoring to censor community theater?

"Shakespeare's R&J" denigrates Catholicism as repressive, the 40 would-be censors claimed, and, to boot, they were offended that two young women kissed on stage. I wonder what they thought of 16-year-old Romeo and Juliet committing suicide? Maybe someone should have grabbed the bard's quill.

Similarly, the Meriden library had been operating under a misguided policy of declining to show art "judged inappropriate or offensive to any segment of the community." It was in direct conflict with the principles of the American Library Association, which states that freedom of expression "is an inalienable human right" and "vital to the resistance of oppression."

The library board eventually tossed out any language about rejecting "offensive" art, but has failed to approve a final policy. In the meantime, artists can't exhibit, a terrible example to our youth of stifling the First Amendment. The board should stop dallying and adopt a new, enlightened exhibit policy.

A century ago, the great Irish writer James Joyce was arguing with his publisher, who wanted him to tame some language and even toss out one offending story in *Dubliners*, his first collection of short stories. Joyce would have none of it. "I cannot alter what I have written," he said. Had he listened to "all these objections I would not have written the book. . . . I cannot write without offending people."

Happily, in Cheshire some local officials understand the importance of free expression. Town Councilor Diane Visconti said she attended the play and saw it as "the passion of youth meeting the passion of Shakespeare." She emphasized: "I don't want to see art so sanitized that it's not interesting."

Town Manager Michael Milone did not succumb to pressure. The message of those offended by the play was "very clear":

'Don't let the play go on'," he said. But he couldn't stop the play any more than he could silence the protests against it.

The study sponsored by the Knight Foundation offers some hope. Seventy percent of the students believe musicians can sing songs that others may find offensive. Let's try to reach the other 30 percent.

Writers, actors, musicians and artists enrich society when they are free to follow their muse.

February 13, 2005

Words, language, clarity and precision

WALLINGFORD SCHOOL SUPERINTENDENT Kenneth V. Henrici and three school board members take the *Record-Journal* to task today for using the words "mentally retarded" in an article last week. They are either disappointed or appalled and want to set the record straight in letters on this page that they never used such words, though the newspaper's coverage made it look like they did.

They ask us to use more "appropriate" terms like students with "special needs."

Earlier letter writers chastised Wallingford educators for using the words "mentally retarded."

In choosing to use the more precise "mentally retarded" and attribute it to Mr. Henrici and board members—when they were using other terms—we erred and we are sorry. We shouldn't put words in people's mouths, especially words they personally eschew. It is difficult, however, to quote officials speaking about students with "special needs" and at the same time inform our readers what they mean by that.

The school board met last week with a state official over how well the district is doing in placing mentally retarded students in classrooms with students of normal intelligence. It is an important issue and needs to be communicated clearly.

From where I sit, too many educators are running amok with political correctness. Their intent is to be kind, I think, but it is misguided kindness.

What is a "special needs" student? Is it a student who can't see the blackboard, so should sit in the front row? Is it a student with cerebral palsy and needs a wheelchair? Is it a brilliant student who needs accelerated learning opportunities? Is it a mentally retarded student who needs a slower pace so he or she can learn?

Why is it offensive to call someone what they are? I would suggest it is offensive, even insulting, to try to mask what someone is, to try to hide what someone is. There is nothing wrong with being mentally retarded, just as there is nothing wrong with being blind. It is not anyone's fault that he or she is mentally retarded.

News articles accurately describing students as mentally retarded in no way mock them. Even the settlement agreement in federal court, which guides all school districts on this issue, states specifically it was a class action lawsuit brought by "All mentally retarded school age-children in Connecticut."

Writers and editors are trained and educated to be precise in choosing words. We try not to use fuzzy language. We have a responsibility to readers to make things clear, to help them understand whatever it is we are writing about.

William Zinsser, who wrote the seminal *On Writing Well*, states in his chapter on "Simplicity" that "we are a society strangling in unnecessary words, circular construction, pompous frills, and meaningless jargon. The airline pilot who announces that he is presently anticipating experiencing considerable precipitation wouldn't dream of saying that it may rain."

Unfortunately, the educational bureaucracies are far too caught up in this cauldron of miscommunication.

Meeting with Greenwich school administrators about their skill as writers, Zinsser persuaded them to change a memo from "Evaluative procedures for the objectives were also established based on acceptable criteria" to "We will see how well we have succeeded."

As newspaper editors and writers we discuss word usage every day. In describing people with low IQs, we have used and continue to use "mentally retarded." Indeed, it remains the Connecticut Department of Mental Retardation. It is not the Connecticut Department of Special Needs.

Some have suggested wording like "mentally handicapped" or "mentally challenged" is better, but I am not at all sure such verbiage is correct.

In fact, the court settlement went on to point out this distinction: "No student will lose his status as a class (action) member due to the renaming or relabeling of his/her disability from 'mental retardation' to 'intellectual disability'," which I take to mean that no amount of euphemism can change the importance of educating the mentally retarded.

It is true language grows and changes. It was once Negro, but is now black or African American. It was once cripple, but is now handicapped—softer, but it fails to say how a person is handicapped.

We don't always hit it right in putting one word after another, but we try for precision and clarity. That is what we owe our readers.

February 16, 2005

⁞ Call me a relic ...

AS THE UNIVERSITY of Connecticut released a survey last Monday showing that only 14 percent of Americans could cite freedom of the press as a right guaranteed by the First Amendment, Connecticut State Historian Walter Woodward lamented the loss of civic education.

An unintended consequence of watering down history with economics and other social sciences has been "to diminish the teaching of our fundamental freedoms," Professor Woodward told a UConn forum on the First Amendment. The good news, he said, is that educators are beginning to focus again on U.S. history, which means students will learn more about our Bill of Rights.

I was glad to hear that. And I'm optimistic enough to think that more than 14 percent of our readers know the First Amendment protects a free press—because we've been writing about it here since 1992.

What is even more heartening is that more than 90 percent of the respondents found it "important" or "essential" for citizens to be able to: speak freely, worship (or not) freely, be informed by a free press, assemble or protest, and petition the government—which ticks off the five freedoms of the First Amendment. So even if we can't identify which amendment protects which rights, we grasp their importance to our free society.

There's even more good news: Those saying that a free press is "essential" to democracy rose from 60 percent in 1997 to 70 percent today. Free speech is essential to 80 percent, up from 72 percent.

Free speech includes singing, and teenagers are way ahead of adults on this. Fifty-eight percent of adults agree that musicians should be able to sing songs with lyrics that might offend others. Fully 70 percent of high school students say that free speech protects singers and songwriters.

That's not surprising, actually, if you remember what your

parents thought of Elvis or Janis Joplin. I was fortunate to have a unique and wonderful mother who danced with her young husband to the big bands. When I was a teen, she told me she was born too early—that my music was better than hers. I'm still stuck there and subscribe to the Bob Seger school:

> *Call me a relic, call me what you will*
> *Say I'm old-fashioned, say I'm over the hill*
> *Today's music ain't got the same soul*
> *I like that old time rock n' roll*

And don't censor it! I don't think much of rap, but don't censor it either!

But back to the news. The UConn survey sadly reports that only about one-third of Americans think the news media report news without bias, while nearly two-thirds see bias.

I'll leave you with this: No one told the American media, after two centuries of a highly partisan press, they must become "objective." The press itself decided. In 1922 the American Society of Newspaper Editors adopted "A Statement of Principles," which declared, "Every effort must be made to assure that the news content is accurate (and) free from bias."

I think some readers confuse the editorial pages and columnists, which are supposed to have clear opinions, with the news pages where we try our best to eliminate opinion. In the growing Internet blogosphere and on most of talk radio, as Professor Woodward put it, "The quality of discourse in this country is a bipartisan disgrace."

We shouldn't censor anyone, but we should be aware of the difference between purveyors of opinion—a blogger or a talk show host—and a newspaper reporter. Most of us in the print media strive for fairness and accuracy in reporting the news. Under the First Amendment, we have the right to print what we please. Under our written principles, we try to paint a full picture.

May 22, 2005

The Bill of Rights
Amendments 1-10 of the Constitution

The Conventions of a number of the States having, at the
time of adopting the Constitution, expressed a desire, in order
to prevent misconstruction or abuse of its powers, that further
declaratory and restrictive clauses should be added, and as
extending the ground of public confidence in the Government
will best insure the beneficent ends of its institution;

Resolved, by the Senate and House of Representatives of the
United States of America, in Congress assembled, two-thirds of
both Houses concurring, that the following articles be proposed
to the Legislatures of the several States, as amendments to the
Constitution of the United States; all or any of which articles, when
ratified by three-fourths of the said Legislatures, to be valid to all
intents and purposes as part of the said Constitution, namely:

Amendment I

Congress shall make no law respecting an establishment of religion,
or prohibiting the free exercise thereof; or abridging the freedom
of speech, or of the press; or the right of the people peaceably to
assemble, and to petition the government for a redress of grievances.

Amendment II

A well regulated militia, being necessary to the security of a free state,
the right of the people to keep and bear arms, shall not be infringed.

Amendment III

No soldier shall, in time of peace be quartered in any
house, without the consent of the owner, nor in time of
war, but in a manner to be prescribed by law.

Amendment IV

The right of the people to be secure in their persons, houses,
papers, and effects, against unreasonable searches and seizures, shall
not be violated, and no warrants shall issue, but upon probable cause,
supported by oath or affirmation, and particularly describing the
place to be searched, and the persons or things to be seized.

Amendment V

No person shall be held to answer for a capital, or otherwise infamous crime, unless on a presentment or indictment of a grand jury, except in cases arising in the land or naval forces, or in the militia, when in actual service in time of war or public danger; nor shall any person be subject for the same offense to be twice put in jeopardy of life or limb; nor shall be compelled in any criminal case to be a witness against himself, nor be deprived of life, liberty, or property, without due process of law; nor shall private property be taken for public use, without just compensation.

Amendment VI

In all criminal prosecutions, the accused shall enjoy the right to a speedy and public trial, by an impartial jury of the state and district wherein the crime shall have been committed, which district shall have been previously ascertained by law, and to be informed of the nature and cause of the accusation; to be confronted with the witnesses against him; to have compulsory process for obtaining witnesses in his favor, and to have the assistance of counsel for his defense.

Amendment VII

In suits at common law, where the value in controversy shall exceed twenty dollars, the right of trial by jury shall be preserved, and no fact tried by a jury, shall be otherwise reexamined in any court of the United States, than according to the rules of the common law.

Amendment VIII

Excessive bail shall not be required, nor excessive fines imposed, nor cruel and unusual punishments inflicted.

Amendment IX

The enumeration in the Constitution, of certain rights, shall not be construed to deny or disparage others retained by the people.

Amendment X

The powers not delegated to the United States by the Constitution, nor prohibited by it to the states, are reserved to the states respectively, or to the people.